Spotter's Guide

ANIMA

TRACKS & SIGNS

Alfred Leutscher

President of the British Naturalists' Association

Illustrated by Chris Shields

of Wilcock: Riley Graphic Art Ltd

Contents

The editors would like to thank Daphne Hills for her help

Photographs were kindly lent by Alfred Leutscher

Edited by
Jessica Datta
and Rosamund Kidman Cox

Additional illustrations by
Roger H. Coggins
of Wilcock: Riley Graphic Art Ltd
and Andy Martin

First published in 1979 by
Usborne Publishing Limited,
Usborne House,
83-85 Saffron Hill, London EC1N 8RT

Printed in Great Britain

How to use this book

This book is an identification guide to **mammals** and the **tracks** they leave; also included are examples of **birds** and bird tracks. **Signs** of animals are often easier to find than the animals themselves, so this book has a whole section about the signs left by animals to help you discover where the animals are.

What you can see in this book

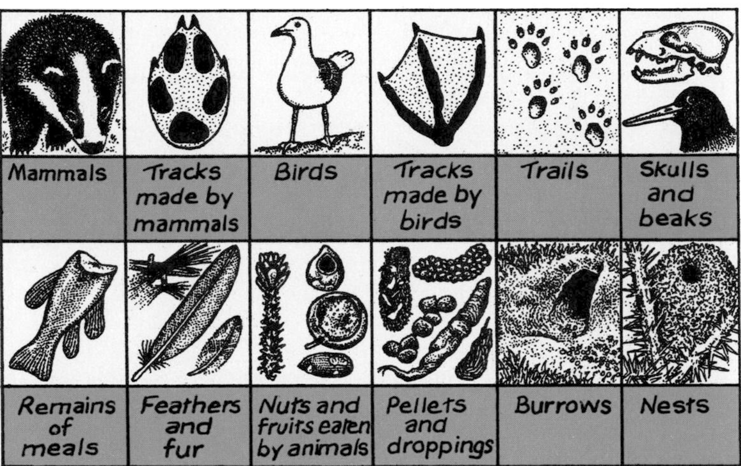

Next to each **picture** of an animal there is a **description** telling you a little about it, where to find it and its **size**. An outline of the **track** made by each animal is next to its picture. On the mammal tracks, the dark brown areas represent the pads and claws and any bright yellow represents webbing between the toes. On the bird tracks, webbing is coloured orange.

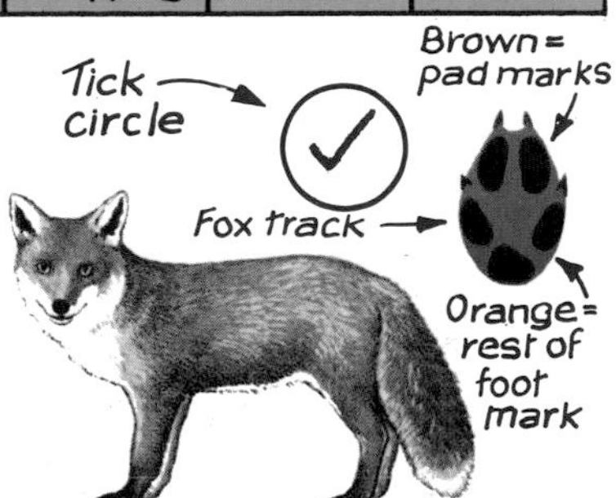

Scoring points

Next to the description of each animal there is a circle. Put a tick in it if you see the animal **or** a track made by the animal. Make sure you have identified your track correctly before you tick it off. Perfect tracks are difficult to find and can easily be confused. Always measure them; this may help you to identify the more difficult tracks.

Now turn to the scorecard at the back of the book to see how many points you have scored. Because many mammals are difficult to spot, score the same for the track as you do for the animal.

Tick circles for animal signs

On the pages about animal signs there are two types of tick circle: a large circle at the top of the page and little circles next to the individual signs. Put a tick in the large circle if you see **any** of the types of signs shown on that page e.g. if you see any droppings or any eaten nuts. You will find general scores for signs in the score card. However, if you actually see one of the signs shown on a page, put a tick in the small circle next to the picture (there are no scores for individual signs). Remember to record in your notebook where and when you saw the sign.

Going abroad

Most of these animals are found in Europe, so you can use this book if you go on holiday abroad. The descriptions will tell you if any of the animals are not found in Britain.

How animals are measured

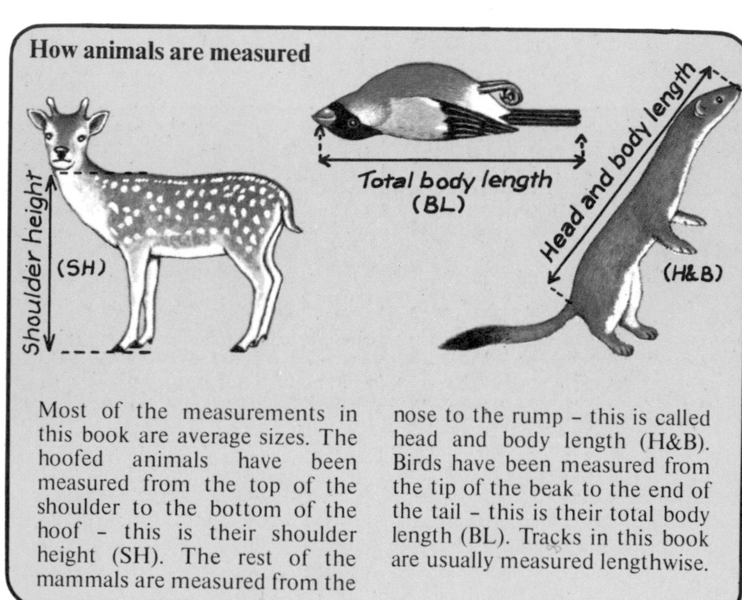

Most of the measurements in this book are average sizes. The hoofed animals have been measured from the top of the shoulder to the bottom of the hoof – this is their shoulder height (SH). The rest of the mammals are measured from the nose to the rump – this is called head and body length (H&B). Birds have been measured from the tip of the beak to the end of the tail – this is their total body length (BL). Tracks in this book are usually measured lengthwise.

What to take when you go out

Wear gumboots and take waterproof clothing which you can kneel on when you are recording tracks. Find yourself a large shoulder bag in which you can carry equipment and your finds. A coat with lots of pockets is useful for carrying the small bits of equipment which you are always using, for example, pencils, note-book, ruler, plastic bags (animal droppings can be messy, so take plenty of bags). Matchboxes lined with cotton wool can be used to carry fragile specimens and an envelope with a piece of card slipped into it will keep feather specimens flat. Carry a penknife in case you need to remove parts of a dead animal, or cut off bits of damaged bark. If at all possible take a camera and binoculars.

Looking for tracks and signs

Recording tracks and signs

Taking photographs is the best way to make records of what you find, but if you have not got a camera take some sheets of clear plastic and a waterproof felt-tip pen when you go out. Place the plastic over any tracks you find and trace over their outlines.

Page 52 tells you how to make plaster casts of tracks. Always write down in your notebook where and when you see any tracks or signs.

Where to look

First of all look for animal paths; they are easy to find and are good places for tracks and droppings. Banks usually have rat or mice paths (called "runs"). You can often find little tunnel "runs" in the undergrowth, in the grass, or under old planks, made by mice or voles.

Mammals often use the same places to cross over banks and hedges and may leave tracks where they have climbed up. If a path runs under a gate or barbed-wire fence, look for bits of hair caught on the wood or wire.

If you know of anywhere muddy, go and investigate; edges of lakes and ponds may have tracks of animals which live there or which go there to drink. Estuaries and mudflats will have lots of bird tracks, but be careful not to get cut off by the tide. Do not wade out onto the mud as you may sink in and get stuck.

The best time of all to look for tracks is after a snow fall. Droppings also show up well in the snow.

Tracks and trails

The tracks shown in this book are perfect ones, but the tracks you will find may be only partly complete, or distorted by thawing snow or uneven ground. You will have to work like a detective, interpreting the patterns and training yourself to look for other clues. The size of the track may confuse you if it has been made by a young animal. Tracks made by fore feet and hind feet may look different and a track made in mud will look very different from one made in snow or in sand.

Always make notes recording the time, place and type of substance the track was made in, and a note of any other signs near the tracks. Below is a small test to start you off. One of the tracks below has been made by a fox and one by a dog. Which is the fox track? The answer is upside-down at the bottom of the page.

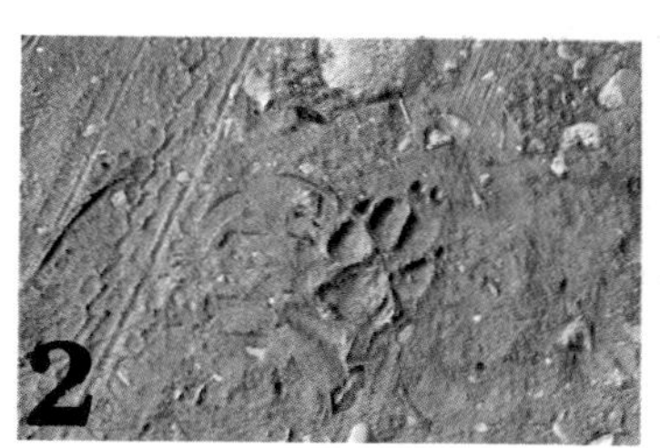

Which is the fox track and which is the dog track?

Bird tracks

Bird tracks are much more difficult to identify than mammal tracks. You will probably be unable to guess the correct species, but you will be able to tell something about the habits of the bird. Swimming birds, like ducks, will leave webbed footprints; wading birds, which walk on mud, will leave tracks with long, slender toes spread wide apart. Perching birds, like crows and sparrows, will leave tracks with a long first toe behind three front toes (this long toe helps them grip onto a perch). When landing in snow, birds leave a wing print; this is made by the long feathers of the wing.

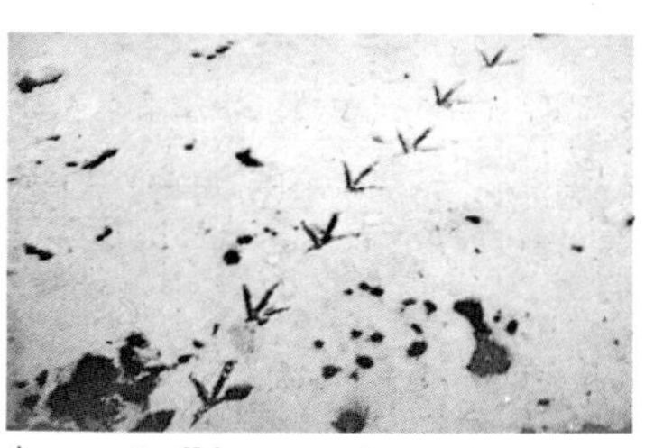

A crow trail in snow ▲

▲ A wing print in snow

Fox=no.1 Dog=no.2

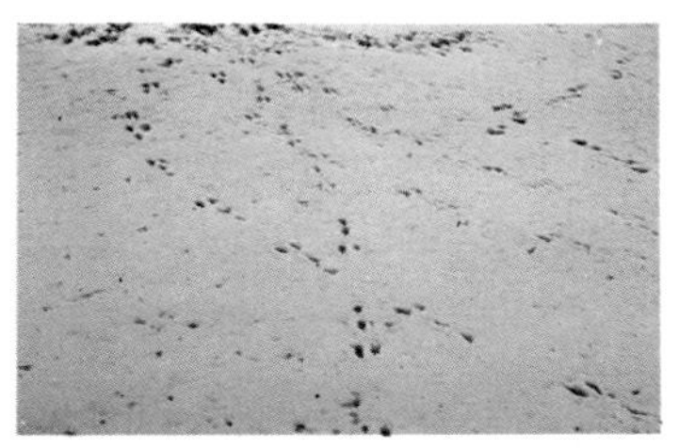

▼ A Rabbit trail in snow ▲

▲ A squirrel trail in snow

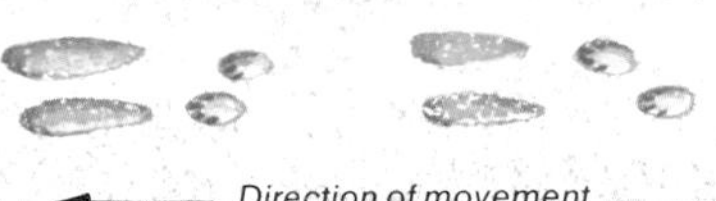

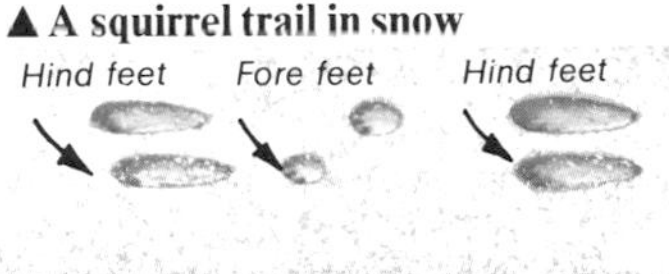

Trails

A trail is a series of tracks made by a moving animal. It may tell you what the animal has been doing and how fast it has been moving.

The rabbit moves by hopping. With each hop it pushes off with its hind feet. It lands first on its fore-feet which touch the ground one in front of the other, the hind feet then touch the ground landing in front of the fore feet. Speed can be worked out by measuring the distance between the groups of tracks; the faster the movement, the greater the gap between groups of tracks.

Snow trails can often be confusing, especially if the snow has started to melt. Above is a photo of a squirrel trail; notice how it looks like the rabbit trail. The squirrel moves in a similar manner, the hind feet landing in front of the fore feet, but you can always recognize a squirrel trail because it will start and finish at the bottom of a tree.

Badger tracks in snow ▲

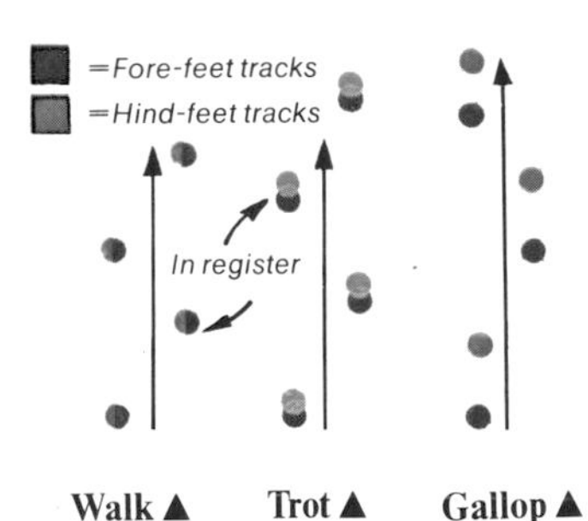

Walk ▲ Trot ▲ Gallop ▲

If the animal has been walking or trotting, the tracks of the trail will be in register. This means that the hind-foot has landed on the track of the fore foot. You can see this in the photo above; it shows a trail made by a walking Badger. A walking animal moves its legs in a definite order. The right fore foot moves first, followed by the left hind food, then the left fore foot is moved, followed by the right hind foot and so on. If an animal has been galloping, the tracks will not be in register.

Deer

Hoofed animals are called ungulates. Most European ungulates, like deer, walk on two toes and leave two-toed tracks; the horse, however, walks on one toe. Deer have branched antlers which they drop after the rut, while cattle, sheep and goats have unbranched horns which are never lost.

Red Deer ►

Lives in herds in open country and woods. In winter, the two sexes live in separate herds. During the October rut, the stag roars. Young calves are spotted. Eats grass, fruit, heather, tree bark. May raid crops. SH 1.5m.

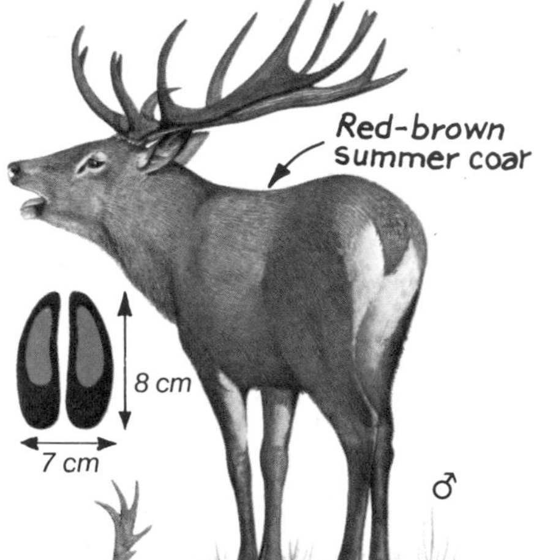

5 cm
6.3 cm
Flattened "palmate" antlers
♂

◄ Fallow Deer

Lives in herds in parks and woods. Buck makes belching grunts during the October rut. Fawns are born in June and are spotted. Eats acorns, grass, berries, bark, fungi. SH 1m.

Muntjac ►

Lives on its own, or in pairs in woods with thick undergrowth. Very quiet, but barks if frightened. Eats mainly wild herbs. SH 50cm.

The two halves of the track are uneven

3 cm

Deer

Roe Deer ►

Red-brown in summer, grey-brown in winter. Lives on its own, or in small groups in conifer wood plantations, near water. The rut is in July/August. Eats leaves, herbs, berries. SH 70cm.

5 cm
4 cm
Tine
There are three tines on each antler
♂

Flattened, palmate antlers
Beard
16 cm
12 cm

◄ Elk/Moose

Largest European deer. In N. and E. Europe. Not in Britain. In woods or marshes. Lives on its own in summer; in winter, lives in herds. Swims well. Eats water plants, grass, moss. SH 1.8m.

5 cm
8 cm
Rarely more than four tines on each antler
♂

Sika Deer ►

Originally from Asia, but found in British woods. Hinds live in small groups. Stags live on their own; the make short, screaming grunts during the October rut. Eats bark, grass, may raid crops. SH 80cm.

Deer, Sheep

Reindeer ►

Coat colour varies; both sexes have antlers. Lives in herds in mountains and tundra of N. Scandinavia; a herd has been introduced into Scotland. Swims well. Hooves make a clacking sound when it is walking. Eats "reindeer moss" (a lichen). SH 1.1m.

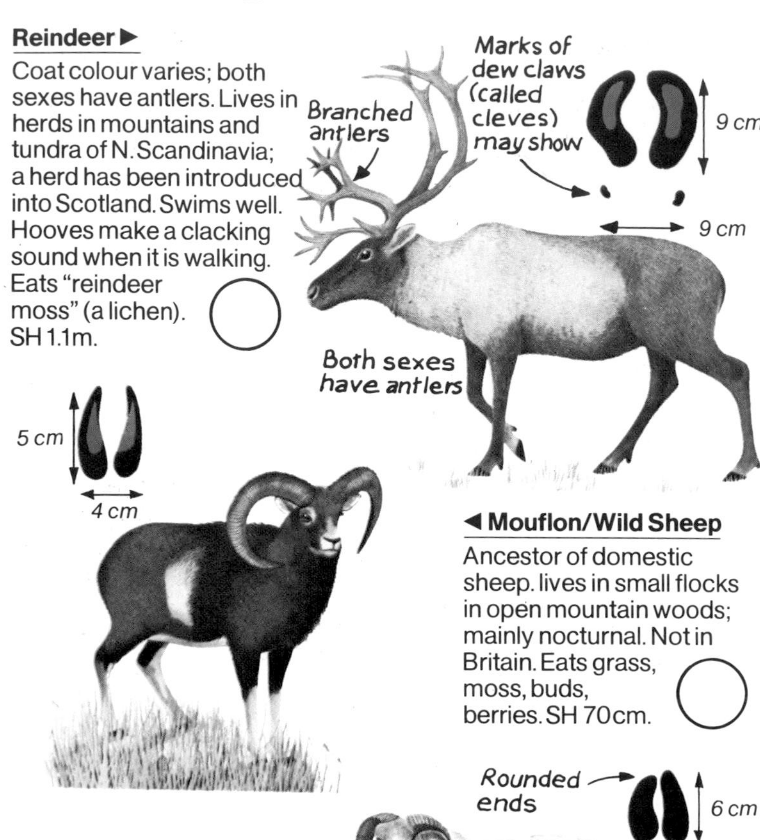

◄ Mouflon/Wild Sheep

Ancestor of domestic sheep. lives in small flocks in open mountain woods; mainly nocturnal. Not in Britain. Eats grass, moss, buds, berries. SH 70cm.

Rounded ends
6 cm
5 cm

Domestic Sheep ►

Many breeds. Kept in fields, open pastures, or mountains. Like its ancestor, lives in flocks with an old ewe as leader. Eats mainly grass. Size varies with breed.

Goats, Chamois

Domestic Goat ▶

Many breeds. Wild on mountains, or domestic on farms. Male is called a billy and usually has a beard. Size varies.

Size varies with the breed

♂

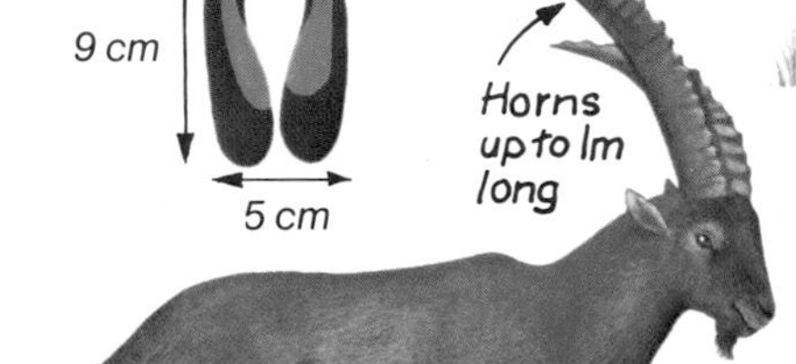

◀ Ibex/Wild Goat

Lives in flocks on high mountains in Europe. Not in Britain. Billy has a beard. Very agile. Eats grass, lichen, moss, leaves. SH 75 cm.

Both sexes have horns

Chamois ▶

Both sexes have horns. Lives in flocks on wooded mountains. Not in Britain. Males live on their own. Very agile. Eats grass, berries, buds. SH 75cm.

Cow, Pigs, Pony

Domestic Cow ►

Colour and size vary with the breed. You may see them with or without horns. Beef cattle may roam free on moors and mountains.

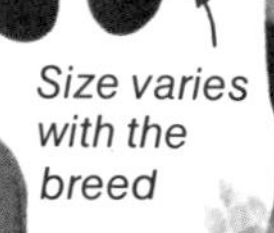

♀

◄ Wild Boar

Ancestor of domestic pig. In woods and marshes of Europe. Not in Britain. Male solitary, females in small groups. Eats roots, bark and fallen fruit such as acorns. SH 90cm.

7 cm

Dew claw

◄ Domestic Pig

Size and colour vary with breed. Kept mainly on farms. When free, eats acorns, beech mast, roots.

Size varies with the breed

Pig hoof

Pony hoof

Exmoor Pony ►

Lives semi-wild in herds on Exmoor. There are other semi-wild ponies in Britain. Eats grass, leaves, low-growing plants.
SH 1.3 m.

Unlike the tracks of pigs, cattle, goats or deer, the pony track is made by one toe

Wolf, Dog, Bear

Carnivores are nearly all flesh eaters (though bears also eat plants). They include the cat, dog, bear and weasel families, all of which have sharp cutting and tearing teeth.

Wolf ►

Usually lives on its own in remote forests in Spain, Scandinavia, Italy and E. Europe. In winter, lives in packs. Eats deer and small mammals. Silent hunter. H&B 1.2m.

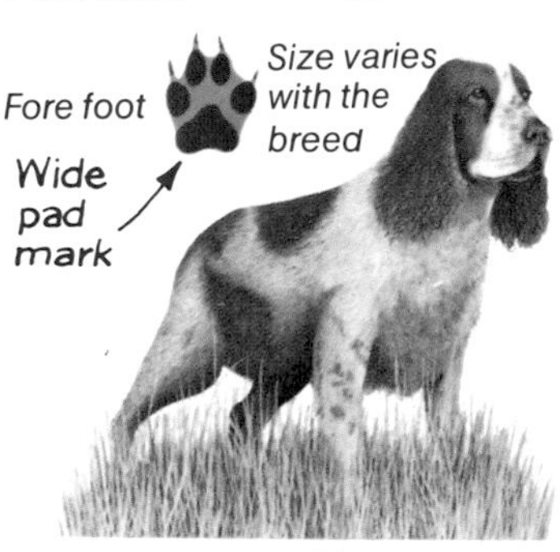

◄ Domestic Dog

Only the Alsatian and Husky can be confused with the wolf. Size and colour vary with the breed. Track has a wide pad mark. Eats mainly meat.

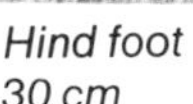

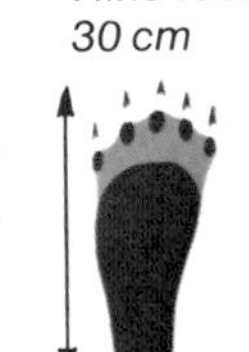

Brown Bear ►

Usually lives on its own in remote areas in Europe. Not in Britain. Nocturnal. Hibernates underground in winter. Omnivorous. H&B 2m.

Foxes, Badger

Red Fox ▶

Common on farmland and in woods, but also on mountains and in towns. Usually nocturnal. Catches small mammals, birds, poultry, young deer.
H&B 65cm.

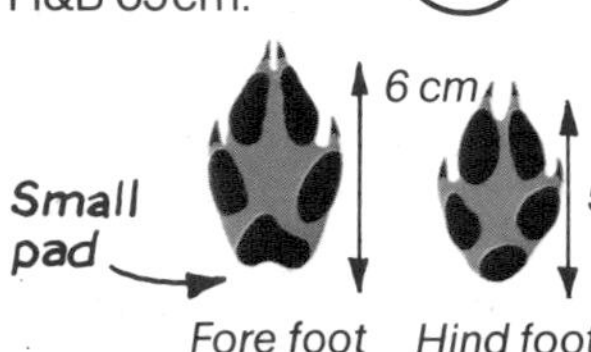

Tracks are 4.5 cm long and similar to those of the Red Fox

◀ Arctic Fox

On tundra and mountains in N. Scandinavia. Not in Britain. Smaller than Red Fox. Coat is dull brown in summer with no white tail tip; usually all white in winter, occasionally grey, Lives in small groups. Active by day and night. H&B 60cm.

Badger ▶

Mainly in woods, but also on mountains. Nocturnal. Lives in a large group in an underground set. Eats mainly worms; also small mammals, insect larvae, wasp nests, plants, roots.
H&B 80cm.

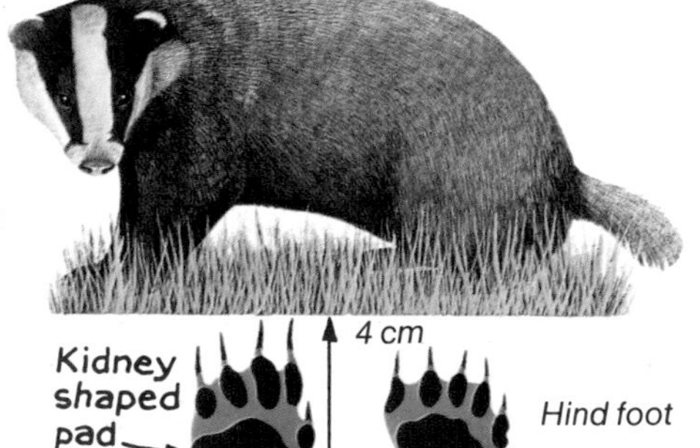

Stoat, Weasel, Mink, Polecat

Stoat ►

Found in woods, farmland and on mountains. Northern stoats, called ermines, are white in winter; tip of tail is always black. Runs with an arched back. Eats rabbits, game birds, eggs. H&B 28cm.

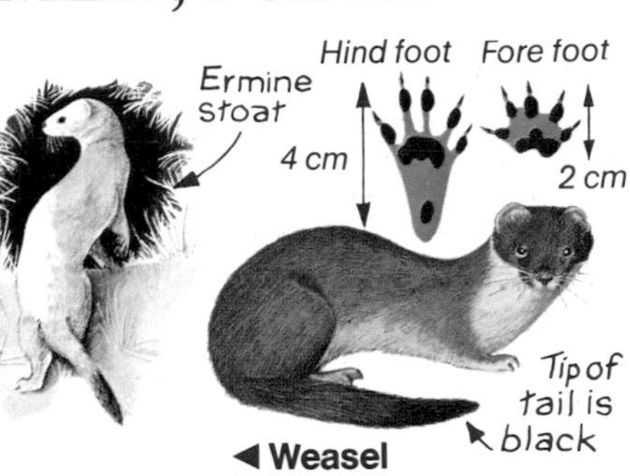

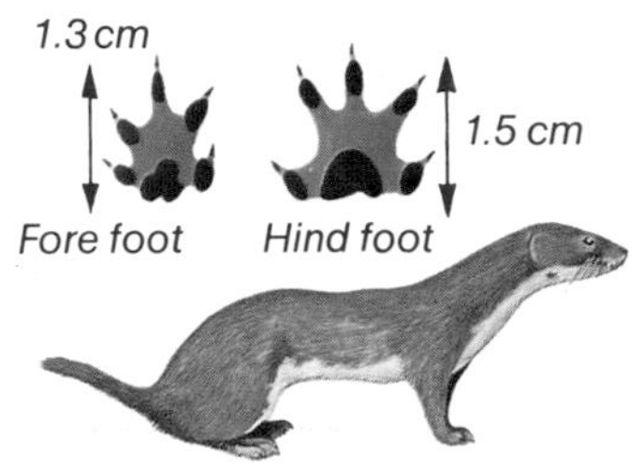

◄ Weasel

Smaller than the stoat; found in similar areas, but prefers dry places. Not in Ireland. Nocturnal and inquisitive. Runs with an arched back. Eats small mammals, birds, eggs. H&B 20cm.

European Mink ►

France and E. Europe. The American Mink has escaped from fur farms in Britain and Europe. Lives near water and swims well. Eats waterfowl, fish, frogs, small mammals, gamebirds, poultry. H&B 38 cm.

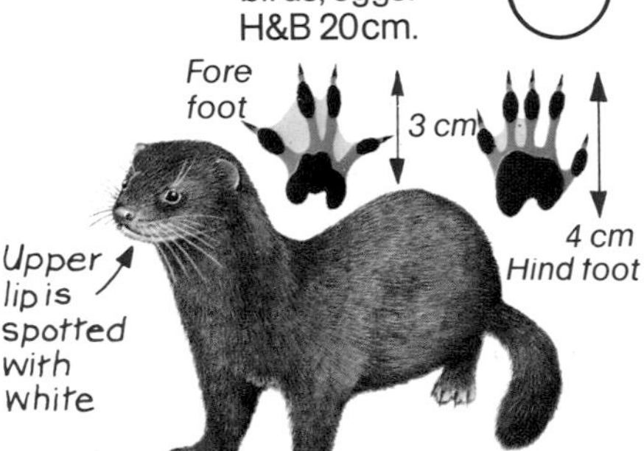

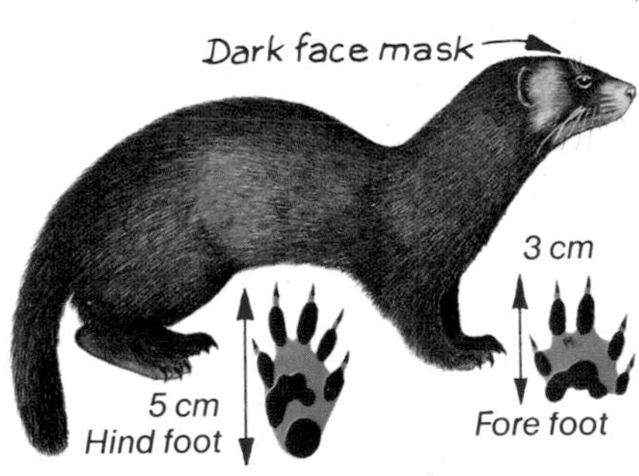

◄ Polecat

Wooded country, often near houses. Rare in Britain. Nocturnal. Tame ones are called ferrets and can be white; they often escape and live wild. Eats frogs, birds, rodents, rabbits. H&B 40 cm.

Otter, Martens

Otter ►

Alongside marshes, rivers, lakes, coastal areas, and on offshore islands. In Britain, found mainly in Scotland. Lives on its own. Nocturnal. Expert swimmer. Eats fish, crabs, frogs, waterfowl, small mammals. H&B 70cm.

◄ Pine Marten

Mountain woods (chiefly conifer woods), away from people. Shy and nocturnal. Good climber. Eats insects, berries, small mammals, birds. H&B 50cm.

Beech Marten ►

In woods and on farmland, often close to houses. Not in Britain. Climbs well. Eats small mammals, birds, sometimes fruit. H&B 45cm.

Cats

Domestic Cat ►

Many breeds. Fed by people, but often hunts small mammals and birds, and may go wild. Active day and night. Size varies.

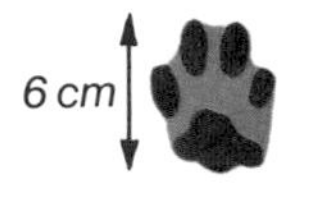

◄ Wild Cat

Larger than domestic cat. Remote woody areas, or among rocks in Scotland and Europe. Nocturnal and shy. Eats mountain animals such as hares, small deer, grouse. H&B 65cm.

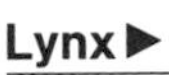

Lynx ►

Scandinavia and E. Europe. Remote mountain woods. Lives on its own. Nocturnal. Eats small mammals, birds, young deer. H&B 1.1m.

Beaver, Coypu, Muskrat

Most rodents are vegetarians and have many chewing teeth. The long, front teeth, called incisors, have sharp edges and are used for gnawing; they wear down easily, but grow continuously to make up for this.

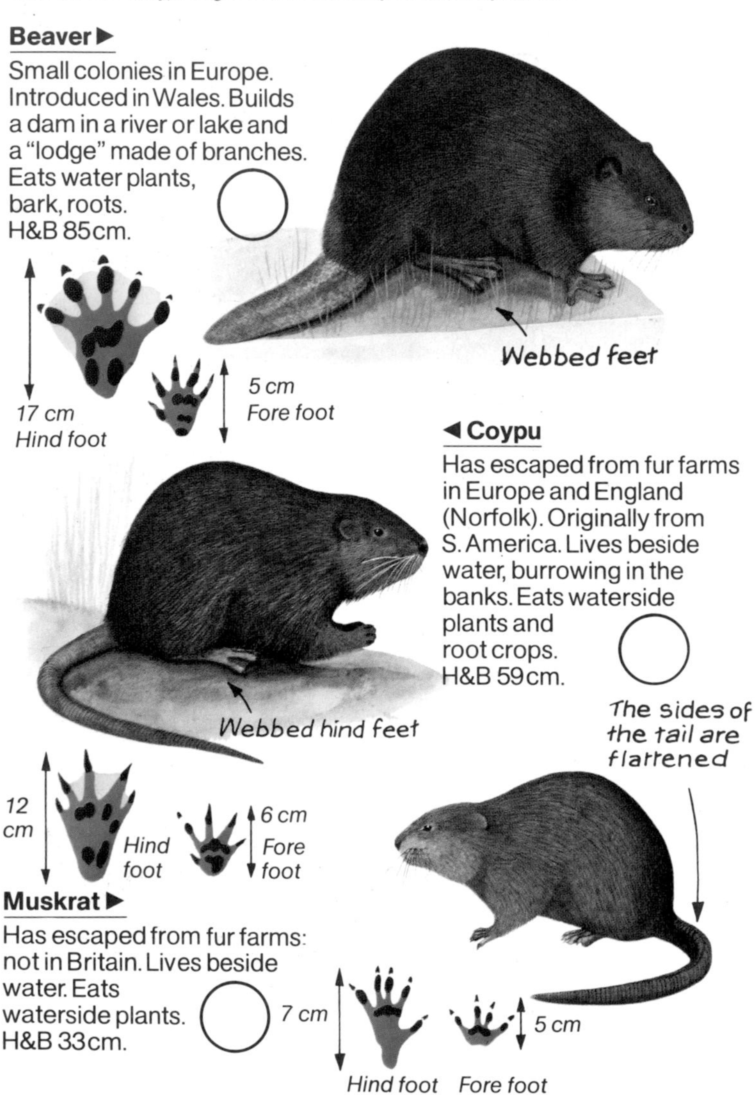

Beaver ▶

Small colonies in Europe. Introduced in Wales. Builds a dam in a river or lake and a "lodge" made of branches. Eats water plants, bark, roots. H&B 85cm.

◀ Coypu

Has escaped from fur farms in Europe and England (Norfolk). Originally from S. America. Lives beside water, burrowing in the banks. Eats waterside plants and root crops. H&B 59cm.

Muskrat ▶

Has escaped from fur farms: not in Britain. Lives beside water. Eats waterside plants. H&B 33cm.

Squirrels, Dormouse

Red Squirrel ▶

Mostly in conifer woods. Active by day, but shy. Eats seeds of cones, berries, buds, bark, birds' eggs, nuts, fungi. H&B 23 cm.

Hind foot 4 cm Fore foot 3 cm

◀ Grey Squirrel

Coat may have patches of brown. Its habits are much the same as the Red Squirrel, but it is bolder and is found in most woods, parks and gardens. H&B 27 cm.

Fore foot 1.5 cm Hind foot 2 cm

Eyes are ringed with black

Edible Dormouse ▶

Introduced in Britain (Hertfordshire). In deciduous woods, parks and orchards. May live near houses, attracted by stored fruit. Nocturnal. Hibernates in winter. Eats nuts, fruit, insects, bark. H&B 12cm.

Dormice, Hamster

Common Dormouse ►

In Britain, lives in heavy undergrowth, copses and hedges. Honeysuckle bark is used to build its hibernation and breeding nests. Nocturnal and solitary; climbs well. Eats insects, berries, seeds, nuts. H&B 8cm.

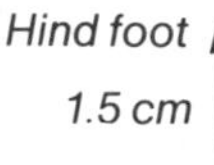

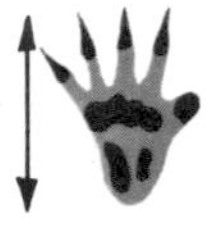

Fore foot
1 cm

◄ Garden Dormouse

Larger, with a more pointed face than the Common Dormouse, but its food and habits are the same. It may enter buildings. Not in Britain or Scandinavia. H&B 13cm.

1.5 cm
1 cm
Hind foot
Fore foot

European Hamster ►

Central Europe on open grassland. Not in Britain. Nocturnal. Lives on its own in a system of burrows. Hibernates. Carries food for storing in its cheek pouches. H&B 27 cm.

Hind foot
Fore foot

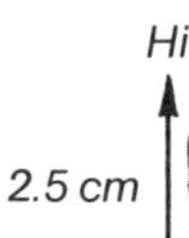

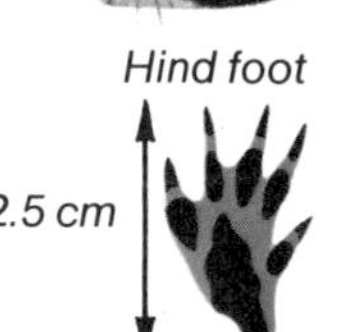

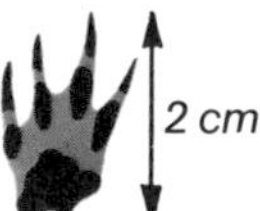

Marmot, Rats

Alpine Marmot ▶

Mountains of Europe. Not in Britain. Active in the day. Lives in a colony in a warren of long tunnels. Has a waddling walk. Sits in an alert position and will give a warning whistle. Eats berries, seeds, nuts, insects.
H&B 55cm.

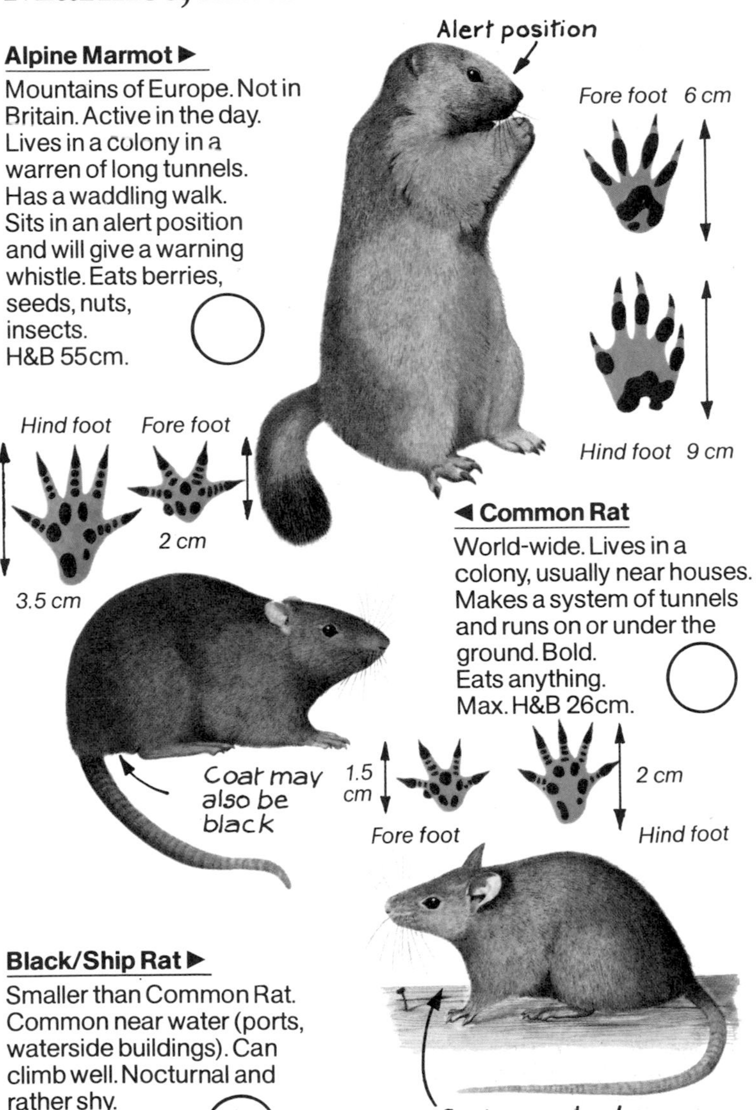

◀ Common Rat

World-wide. Lives in a colony, usually near houses. Makes a system of tunnels and runs on or under the ground. Bold.
Eats anything.
Max. H&B 26cm.

Black/Ship Rat ▶

Smaller than Common Rat. Common near water (ports, waterside buildings). Can climb well. Nocturnal and rather shy.
Eats anything.
Max. H&B 20cm.

Voles, Lemming

Water Vole ►

W. Europe. Not in Ireland. Active by day. Swims well and digs its burrows in the banks of ponds, canals, streams and marshes. Eats waterside plants, worms, snails, fish. H&B 19cm.

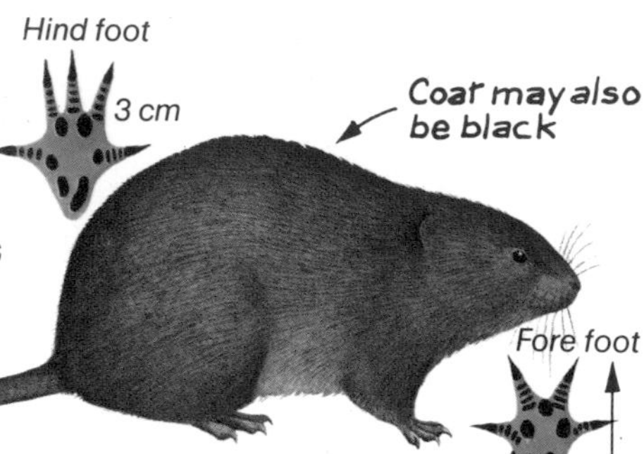

◄ Short-tailed/Field Vole

Not in Ireland. Widespread on open ground. Active by day. Rarely climbs, but makes tunnels through the undergrowth. Eats grass, roots, bark. H&B 11cm.

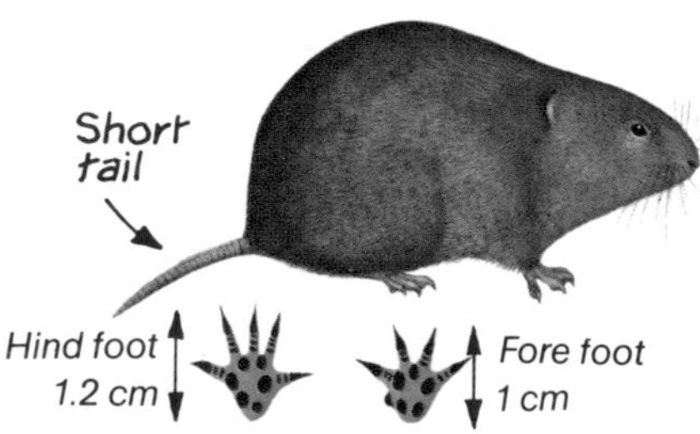

Bank Vole ►

Widespread in deciduous woods and hedgerows. Active by day. Climbs well and makes its burrows in banks. Eats buds, berries, insects, bark. H&B 10cm.

◄ Norway Lemming

Lives in colonies, usually on mountains. Not in Britain. Migrates in large groups every two or three years. Eats berries, grass, bark. H&B 14cm.

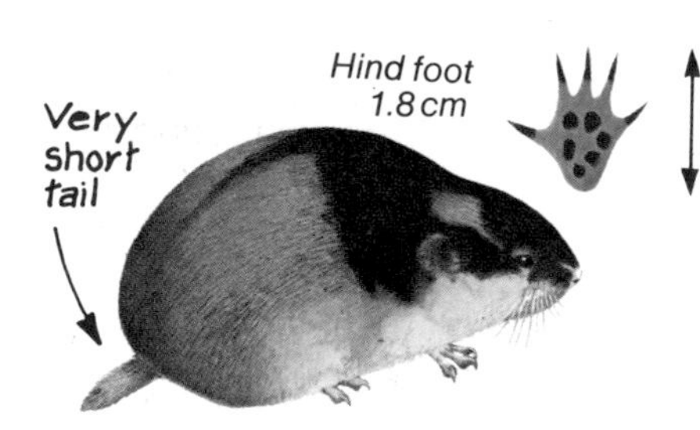

Mice

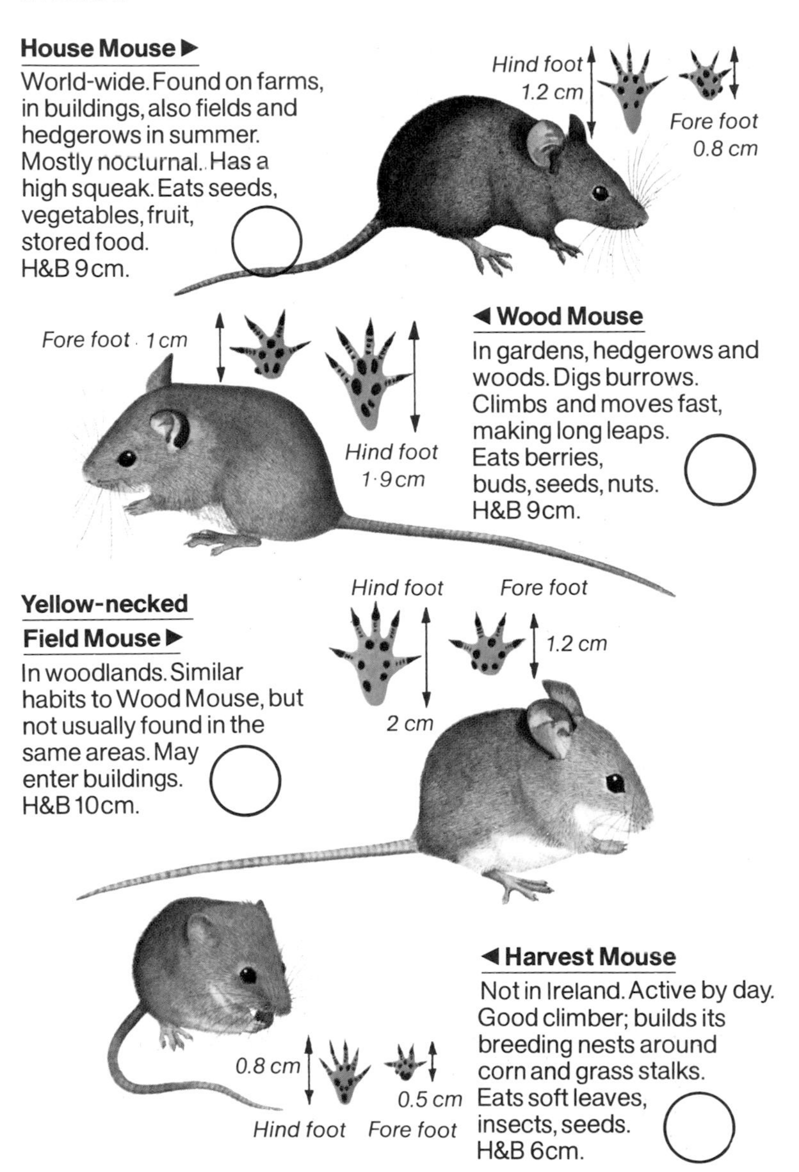

House Mouse ►

World-wide. Found on farms, in buildings, also fields and hedgerows in summer. Mostly nocturnal. Has a high squeak. Eats seeds, vegetables, fruit, stored food. H&B 9cm.

◄ Wood Mouse

In gardens, hedgerows and woods. Digs burrows. Climbs and moves fast, making long leaps. Eats berries, buds, seeds, nuts. H&B 9cm.

Yellow-necked Field Mouse ►

In woodlands. Similar habits to Wood Mouse, but not usually found in the same areas. May enter buildings. H&B 10cm.

◄ Harvest Mouse

Not in Ireland. Active by day. Good climber; builds its breeding nests around corn and grass stalks. Eats soft leaves, insects, seeds. H&B 6cm.

Rabbit, Hares

Rabbit ►

On farm and woodland, sand dunes and hillsides. Lives in colonies in a large burrow system. Active dusk and dawn. Thumps the ground with its hind feet when alarmed.
Eats plants.
H&B 40cm.

Fore foot Hind foot
2.5 cm
12 cm

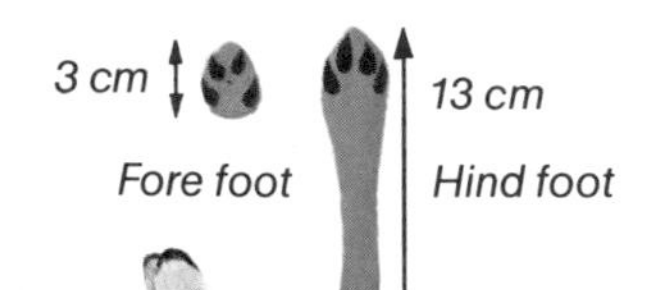

◄ Blue Hare

Mountainous country in Britain, Scandinavia and the Alps. Lives on its own. Active by day and night. Rests above ground and eats mountain plants.
H&B 50cm.

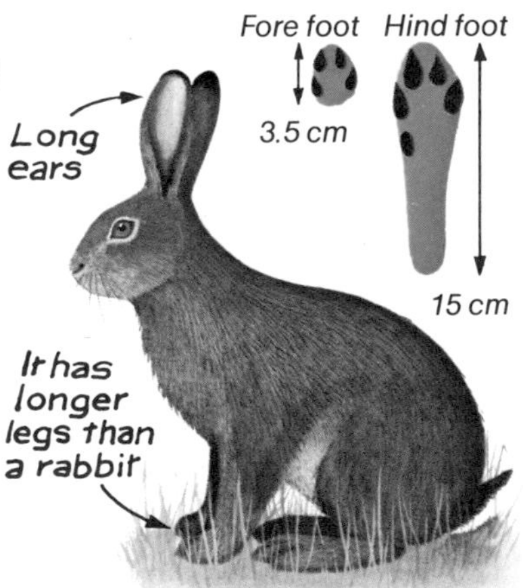

Brown Hare ►

Lives on open farmland and woodland. Not in Norway, Sweden or most of Ireland. Usually solitary and silent. Rests above ground in a hollow ("form").
H&B 58cm.

Seals

When the Grey Seal comes onto land it usually rests on rocks, so you will not see any tracks.

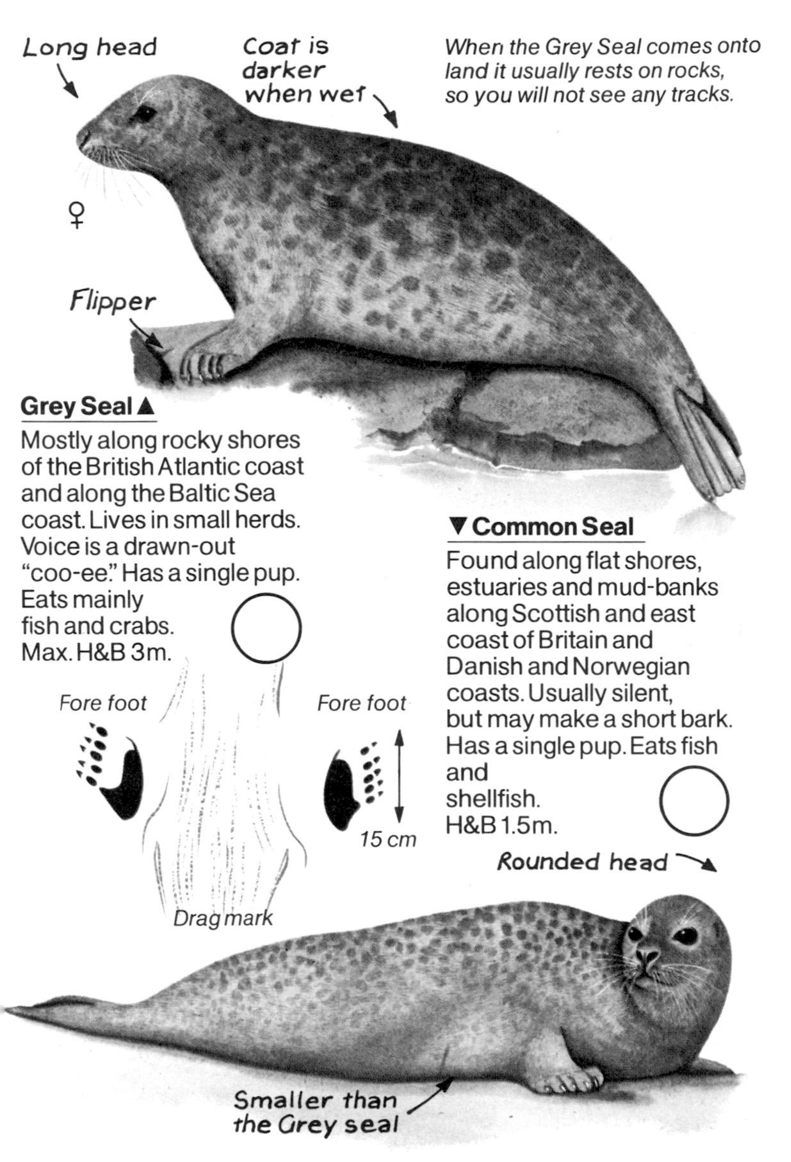

Grey Seal ▲

Mostly along rocky shores of the British Atlantic coast and along the Baltic Sea coast. Lives in small herds. Voice is a drawn-out "coo-ee." Has a single pup. Eats mainly fish and crabs. Max. H&B 3m.

▼ Common Seal

Found along flat shores, estuaries and mud-banks along Scottish and east coast of Britain and Danish and Norwegian coasts. Usually silent, but may make a short bark. Has a single pup. Eats fish and shellfish. H&B 1.5m.

Mole, Hedgehog, Shrew

Mole ►

Lives underground on farms and in woods. Not in Ireland. Does not burrow in sandy or marshy areas. Occasionally comes to the surface. Molehills are piles of waste earth from its tunnels. Sensitive to vibrations. Eats grubs, earthworms, insects.
H&B 13cm.

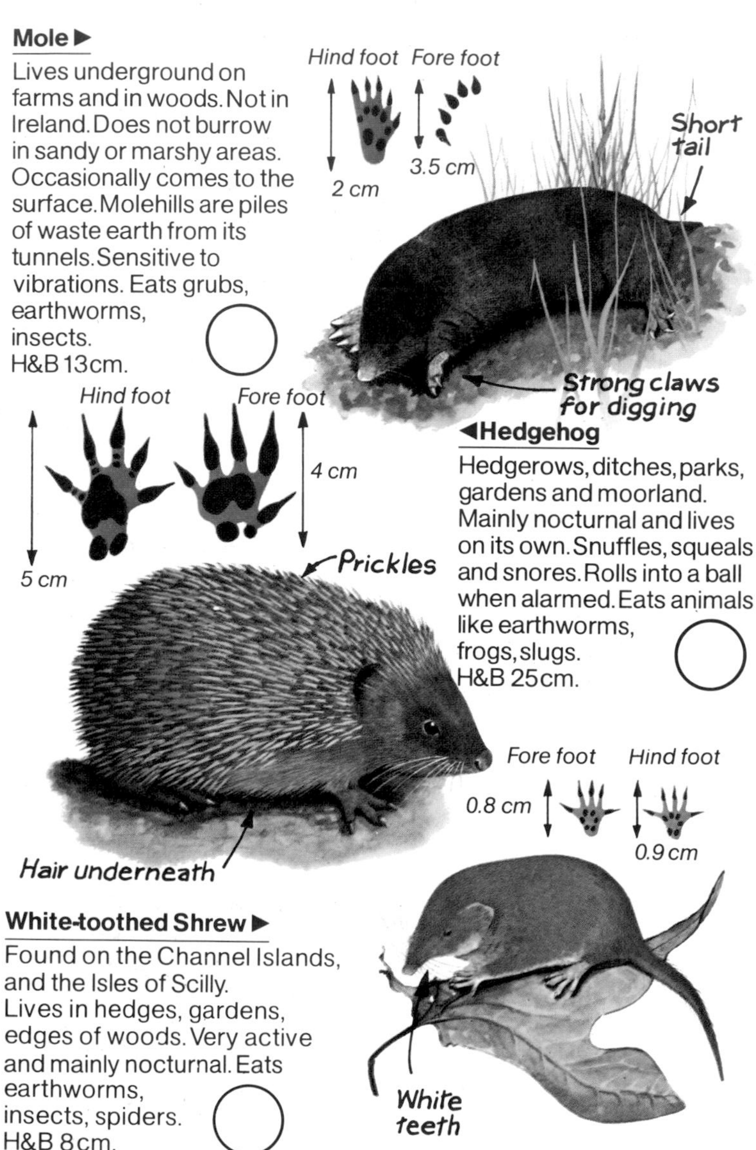

◄Hedgehog

Hedgerows, ditches, parks, gardens and moorland. Mainly nocturnal and lives on its own. Snuffles, squeals and snores. Rolls into a ball when alarmed. Eats animals like earthworms, frogs, slugs.
H&B 25cm.

White-toothed Shrew ►

Found on the Channel Islands, and the Isles of Scilly. Lives in hedges, gardens, edges of woods. Very active and mainly nocturnal. Eats earthworms, insects, spiders.
H&B 8cm.

Shrews

Common Shrew ▶

Rough pasture, woods, hedgerows, dunes and marshes. Not in Ireland. Climbs and swims. Has a high, shrill squeak. Very quarrelsome. Eats insects, worms. H&B 7cm.

Hind foot 0.9 cm *Fore foot 1 cm*

Tips of the teeth are red

Grey-white fur underneath

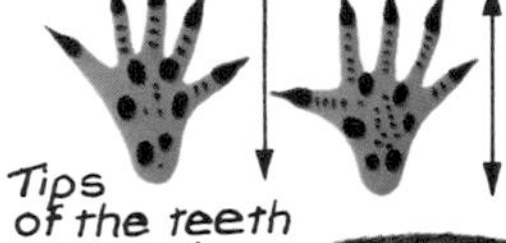

Tips of the teeth are red

◀ Water Shrew

Not in Ireland. Lives close to water; makes tunnels in the banks. A good swimmer; active day and night. Eats small fish, worms, insects. H&B 8cm.

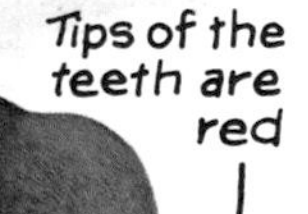

Pygmy Shrew ▶

In dry undergrowth of hedges, young conifer woods, heather and rough pasture. Habits are similar to those of the Common Shrew. H&B 5 cm.

Hind foot *Fore foot*

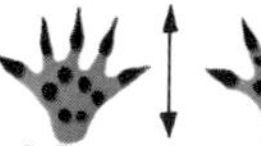

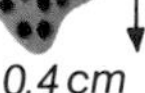

0.5 cm *0.4 cm*

Grebe, Cormorant, Heron

Great Crested Grebe ►

Seen on open water, such as lakes and reservoirs. Sits low on the water and dives often. Builds a floating nest. Eats fish, water insects.
BL 48cm.

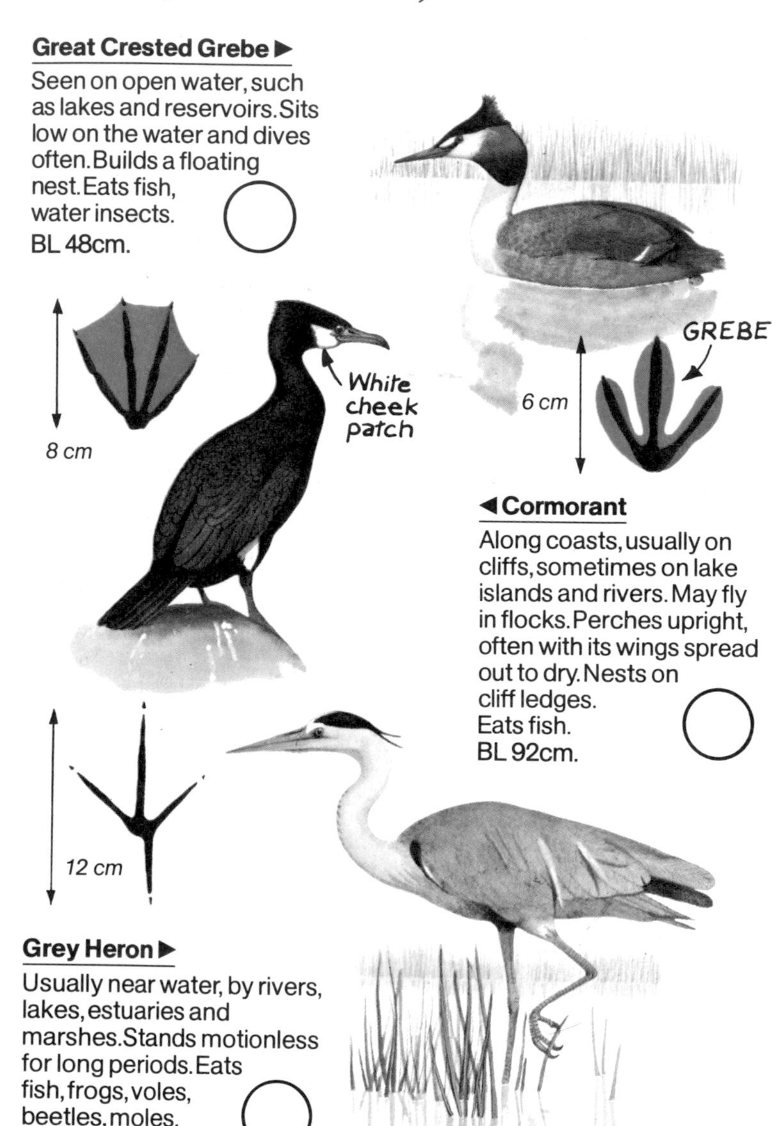

◄ Cormorant

Along coasts, usually on cliffs, sometimes on lake islands and rivers. May fly in flocks. Perches upright, often with its wings spread out to dry. Nests on cliff ledges.
Eats fish.
BL 92cm.

Grey Heron ►

Usually near water, by rivers, lakes, estuaries and marshes. Stands motionless for long periods. Eats fish, frogs, voles, beetles, moles.
BL 92cm.

Goose, Duck, Pheasant

Greylag Goose ►

Nests in Scotland and some breed further south. European birds may be seen near the coast. Lives in flocks which fly in a V formation. Nests on the ground. Eats grass, sometimes water plants. BL 82cm.

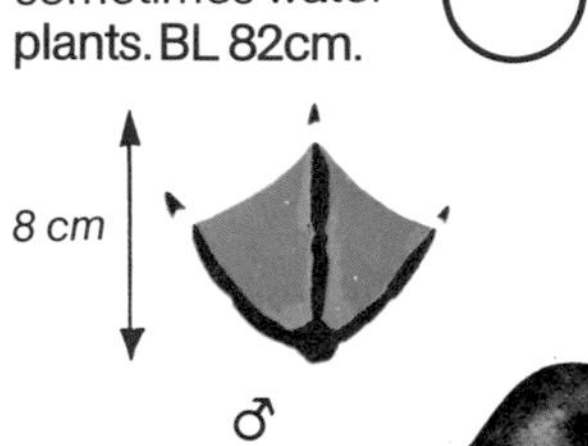

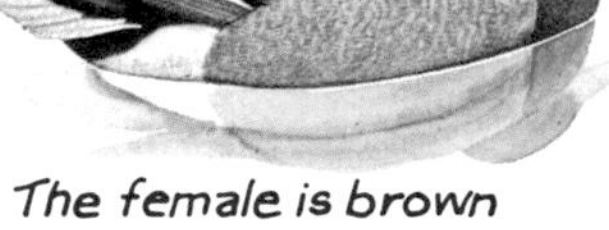

The female is brown

◄ Mallard

Female is mottled brown with a purple wing patch and greenish beak. Common on water. Eats small water plants, sometimes water insects, snails, worms. BL 58cm.

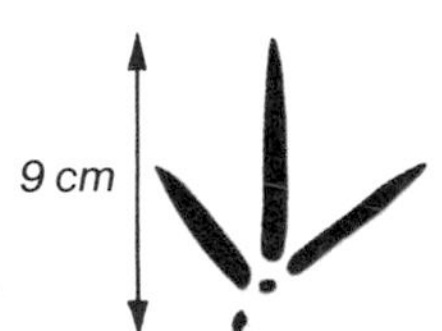

Pheasant ►

A game bird. Feeds and nests on the ground in woods and farmland. Eats grain, insects, worms. Male BL 87cm, female BL 58cm.

The female is brown

Coot, Moorhen, Curlew

Moorhen ▶

On ponds, marshes, streams. Swims with a jerky movement. Nests among reeds. Eats water plants, fruit, seeds, insects, worms, slugs. BL 33cm.

◀ Coot

Usually in groups on lakes and reservoirs. Bobs its head when swimming. Nests among reeds or water plants. Eats water plants, some insects. BL 38cm.

Curlew ▶

On mudflats, estuaries, coasts; inland in summer. Nests on marshes, moors, sand dunes. Flies fast and high in large flocks. Eats insects, worms, berries, sea worms, crabs, small fish. BL 55cm.

Gull, Sparrow, Rook

Herring Gull ▶

This is the most common gull on sea coasts. It nests on rocky cliffs. You may also see it inland feeding on ploughed fields. It has a distinctive, loud call which sounds like "kyow." Feeds on shellfish, eggs, chicks, fish, edible scraps.
BL 56cm.

◀ House Sparrow

Common in towns and on farmland. May nest in buildings. Hops on the ground and roosts in flocks. Eats mainly seeds and kitchen waste.
BL 15cm.

Grey beak (the Crow has a black beak)

Bare area on the face

5 cm

Rook ▶

On farmland, usually in flocks. The group of nests, usually in tall trees, is called a rookery. Feeds on ploughed ground and eats insects, grubs, grain.
BL 46cm.

There are feathers on the thighs

Mammal skulls

Below are some of the different types of skulls you may see. If you find a dead animal and do not want to boil it up to remove the flesh, bury it in the garden. Wait about six months until decomposition has removed most of the flesh. Then dig it up and clean the bones.

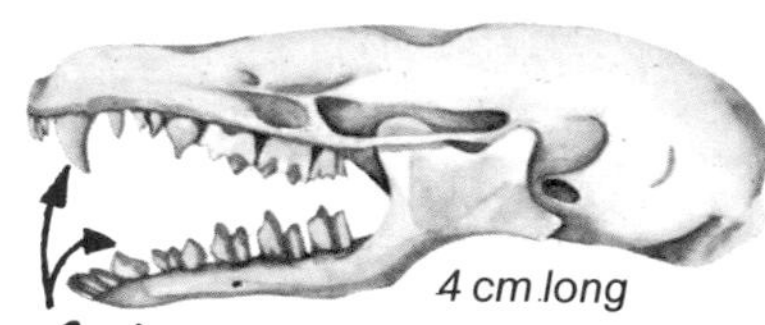

▲ Mole. Insect eater. Notice the long muzzle and all the sharp chewing teeth. The skull may be found in owl pellets.

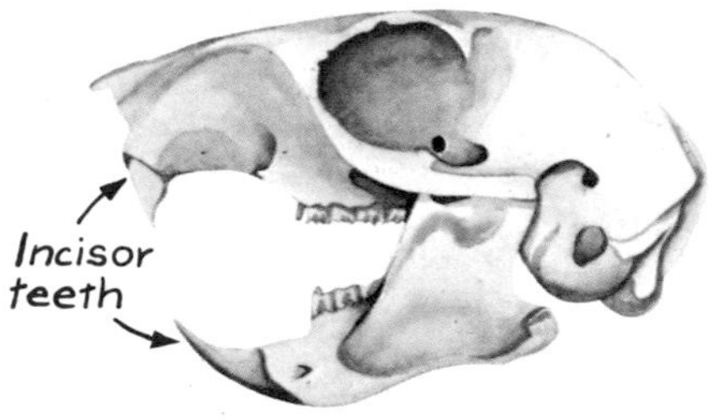

◀ Grey Squirrel. Rodent. Has strong front incisor teeth used for gnawing and biting hard plant material.

Badger ▶ Meat eater. Notice the long canine teeth and the sharp chewing teeth. Strong jaw muscles are attached to the ridge on top of the skull.

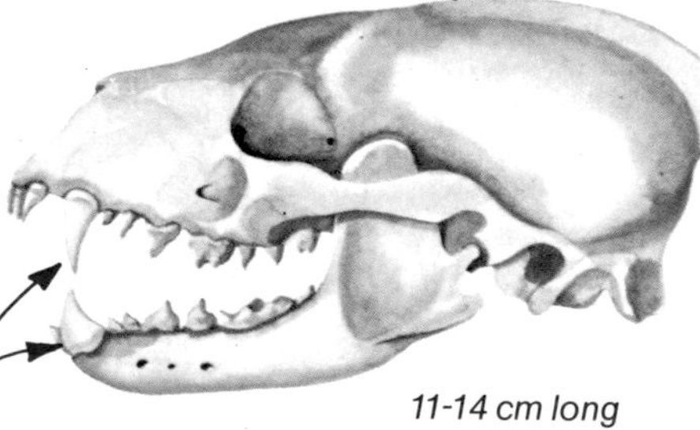

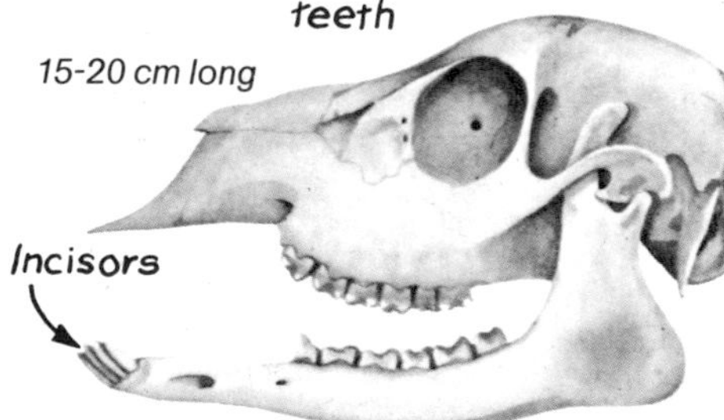

◀ Roe Deer. Plant eater. The long incisor teeth are used for biting off bits of plants and the flat molar teeth for chewing them.

Bird beaks

If you find a bird skull, or a dead bird, the shape of the beak will tell you what sort of food the bird ate, and therefore what group of birds it belonged to.

▲ **Tawny Owl.** Meat eater. All birds of prey have hooked beaks used for tearing meat.

Hawfinch ▲ Seed eater. All finches have strong, stubby beaks used for cracking open seeds and nuts.

Sharp, stabbing beak

▲ **Green Woodpecker.** Insect eater. Has a long, sharp, strong beak used for probing for and picking up insects and chipping wood.

Reed Warbler ▲ Insect eater. Has a thin, pointed beak used for catching flying insects.

Long beak

▲ **Oystercatcher.** Feeds on animals that live in mud. Has a long, powerful beak that can probe for and force open shells.

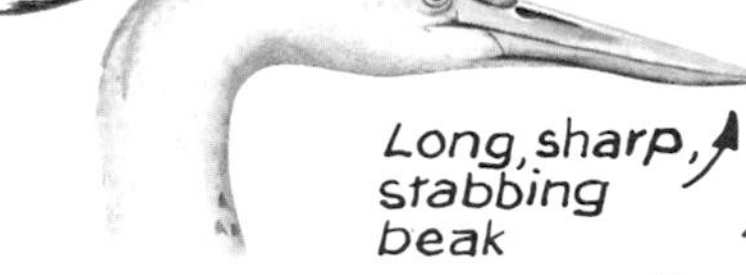

Grey Heron ▲ Fish eater. Has a long, sharp beak used for stabbing fish and water animals.

Flat beak

▲ **Mallard.** Tiny plants and animals are caught on the grooves on the margin of the beak as water is passed through the bill.

Fur and feathers

Fur and hairs

Bits of fur or hair can be found in places where the animal has had to squeeze through or under something, usually wood or barbed wire. Fur on the ground may be a sign of a fight or the remains of an animal's meal.

▲ **Badger hairs.** Badgers usually have special paths which often cross under fences. Look for hairs

◀ **Sheep wool.** This is easy to find, usually on barbed wire. It is often in matted lumps.

Feathers

Feathers are easy to find, even in towns, as birds moult at least once a year. Feathers may also be left behind after an animal has eaten a bird. Below are some of the types of feathers you may see.

Meal remains of meat eaters

Most animals eaten by predators are small and are therefore eaten whole. Any remains are usually eaten by other predators such as crows. The most common remains you are likely to see are feathers or fur. If you are lucky and find a half-eaten animal, look for teeth or beak marks which may give you a clue. If the prey is a bird, look at the ends of its feathers; if they are chewed, the predator will have been a mammal. Below are some examples. ○

▲ A **Stoat** kills its prey by biting it on the head. This Rabbit has also had its eyes pecked out by crows. ○

This pigeon was eaten by a **Fox**. ▲ The ends of the wing feathers have been chewed and the bones of the body crushed. ○

▲ A group of broken snail shells on a rock is a sign that a **Song Thrush** has been smashing the snails to get at their soft parts. ○

Birds of prey tear off the head ▲ (they may eat the brain), pluck out the feathers and eat the flesh, especially the breast meat. Beak marks may be left in the flesh. ○

▲ Prey killed by an **Otter** will usually be near water. You may find a fish tail (the head is eaten first) or just a few fish bones and scales. ○

Meal remains of plant eaters

The feeding signs of plant eating animals are much easier to find than those of carnivores. If you have a vegetable garden, examine root crops, such as turnips, beet and potatoes, for signs of rodent feeding. In autumn, examine fallen apples for teeth and beak marks. You are also quite likely to find marks on tree bark. Examine teeth marks carefully; the sizes may help you identify the feeder. There are often tracks or droppings nearby which may also give you a clue. ◯

▲ Bark eaten by Fallow Deer. Deer tear off strips of bark; squirrels and voles also gnaw and strip bark, but they leave smaller tooth marks. ◯

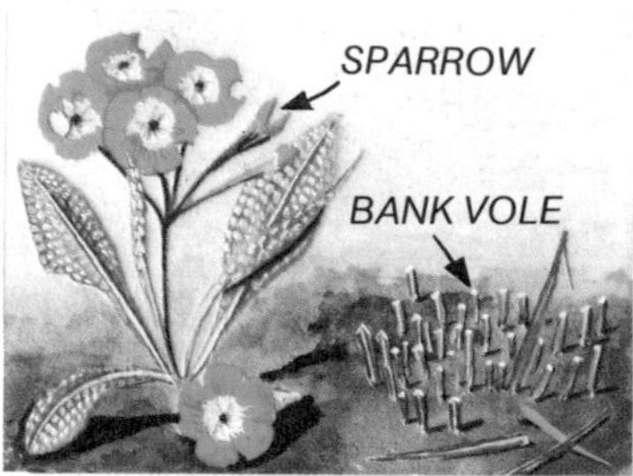

Young plants ▲ Many birds eat young shoots; look for beak marks in the leaves and flowers. Voles leave tooth marks on the shoots. ◯

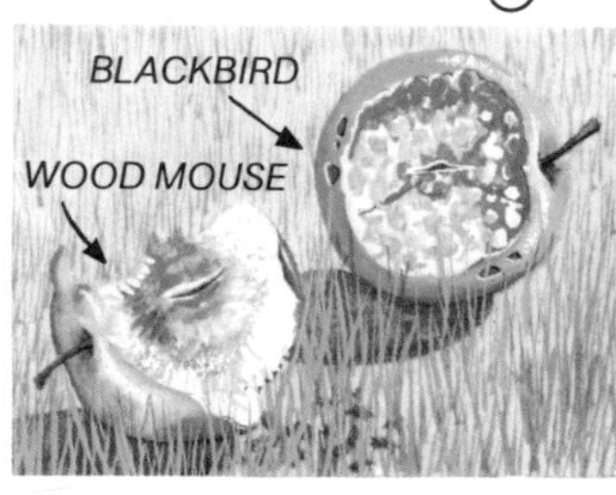

▲ Fruit. The teeth marks of rodents can be seen near the edge of the skin. Look for droppings. Birds will leave peck marks in the flesh. ◯

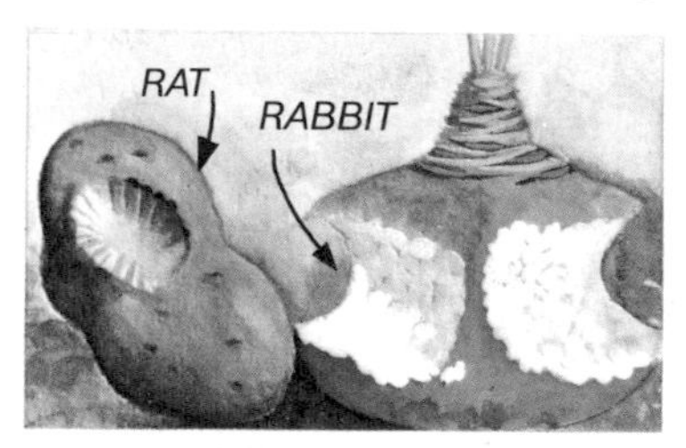

Root crops ▲ Rats and voles eat roots above and below ground. Hares, rabbits and deer eat the parts above ground. ◯

▲ Toadstool eaten by a squirrel. The teeth marks of rodents are very obvious on the flesh. Slugs leave small, round, surface holes. ◯

Cones eaten by animals

Each cone consists of a central stem and overlapping scales. The seeds are at the base of the scales and are ripe in autumn. To get at the seeds, birds lift, tear, or pull back the scales. Rodents usually start at the top of the cone, gnawing off the large scales.

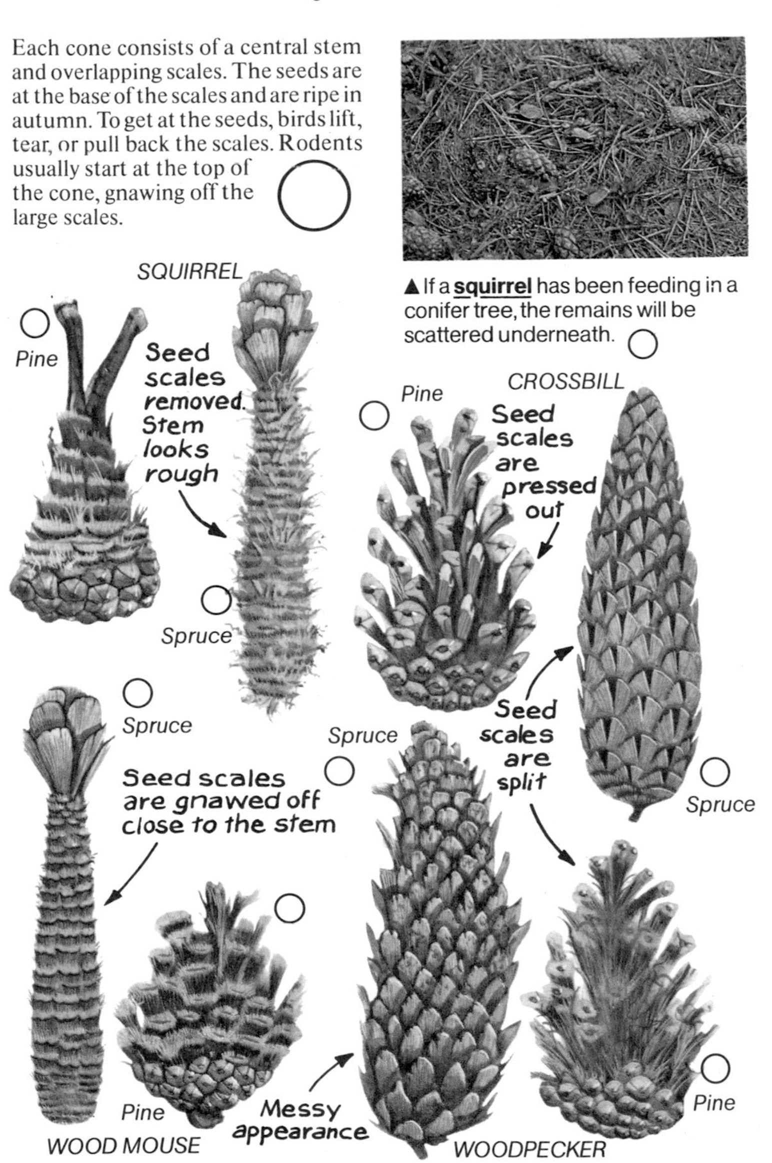

▲ If a **squirrel** has been feeding in a conifer tree, the remains will be scattered underneath.

Nuts eaten by animals

In autumn, look under the trees and bushes that produce nuts, such as Hazel bushes, Chestnut, Walnut and Beech trees. Each animal has a particular way of eating a nut. If you find nut shells, look for teeth or beak marks, and at the shape and edge of the hole or margin. ○

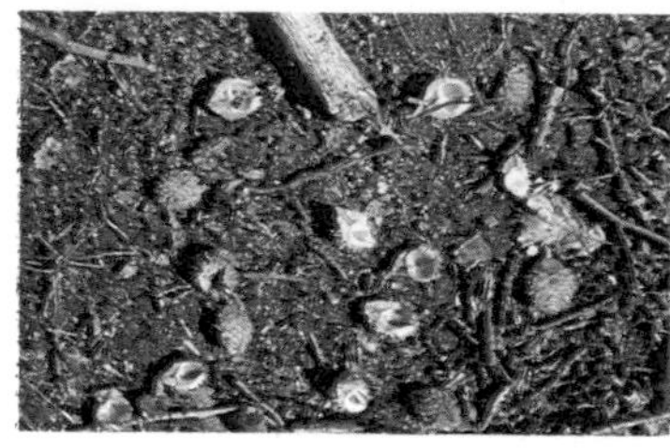

▲This **beech mast** is unripe. Some animal, probably a **squirrel** has bitten them off a branch and eaten the nut kernels inside them. ○

Sweet Chestnut eaten by a RABBIT ○

Marks left by the front teeth

Hazelnut eaten by a a WOOD MOUSE ○

Teeth marks

Walnut eaten by a BLUE TIT ○

It has chipped the shell away to get at the kernel

Hazelnut eaten by a GREY SQUIRREL ○

The shell has been split at the top and gnawed near the base

Hazelnut eaten by a BANK VOLE ○

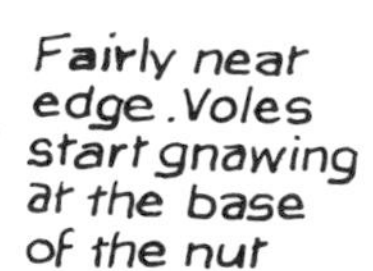

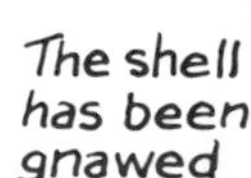

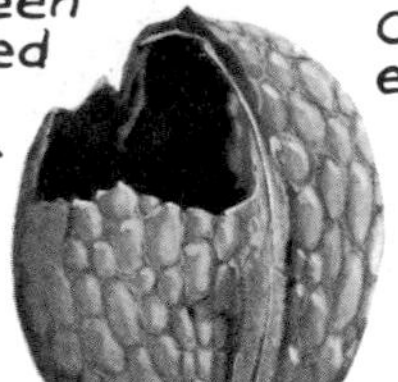

Walnut eaten by a RAT ○

Clean edge

Hazelnut eaten by a DORMOUSE ○

Nuts eaten by animals

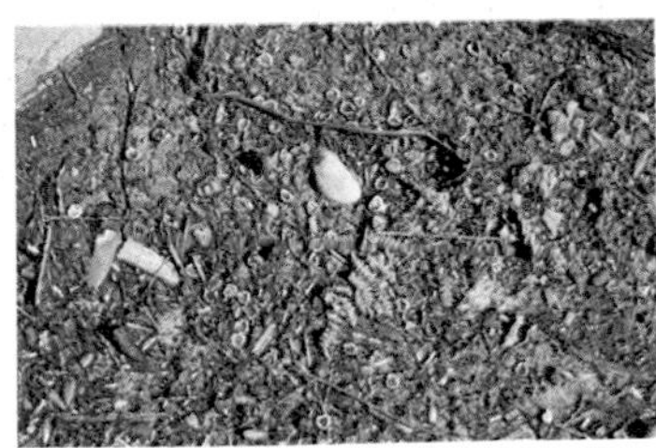

▲ **Finches** have very strong beaks that can crack open nuts. The two halves of the nut will have no beak marks on them. ○

Notice the teeth marks. A Bank Vole would leave no marks

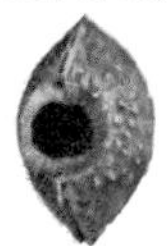

○ *Cherry stone eaten by a WOOD MOUSE*

○

Cherry stones cracked open by a HAWFINCH

Beechnuts eaten by birds are usually found wedged into cracks in bark

Beechnut eaten by a WOODPECKER ○

The edge of the shell shows the teeth marks

Beechnut eaten by a WOOD MOUSE ○

○

Acorn eaten by a WOOD MOUSE

The nut has been wedged into bark and shattered with several blows of the bird's beak

○

Almond cracked open by a WOODPECKER

Almond kernel eaten by a WOOD MOUSE

○

Teeth marks

Notice the marks left by the front teeth

Acorn eaten by a RABBIT

○

Mammal droppings

Animal droppings are easy to find and can tell you a lot about an animal's habits. Write down where you find them; by doing this you may be able to build up a record of the animal's movements and perhaps find out where its home is.

Droppings are made mostly of parts of food that the animal cannot digest, for example, bones, hard parts of insects, hard seeds, and plant fibres. By looking carefully at droppings you can often tell what type of food the animal has been eating. Meat eaters leave sausage-shaped droppings with pointed ends. Plant eaters usually leave small, round droppings.

Some animals–cats for example, dig special holes for their droppings. Rabbits and foxes use droppings to mark out territory; they always leave them in obvious places, such as on molehills or rocks. ◯

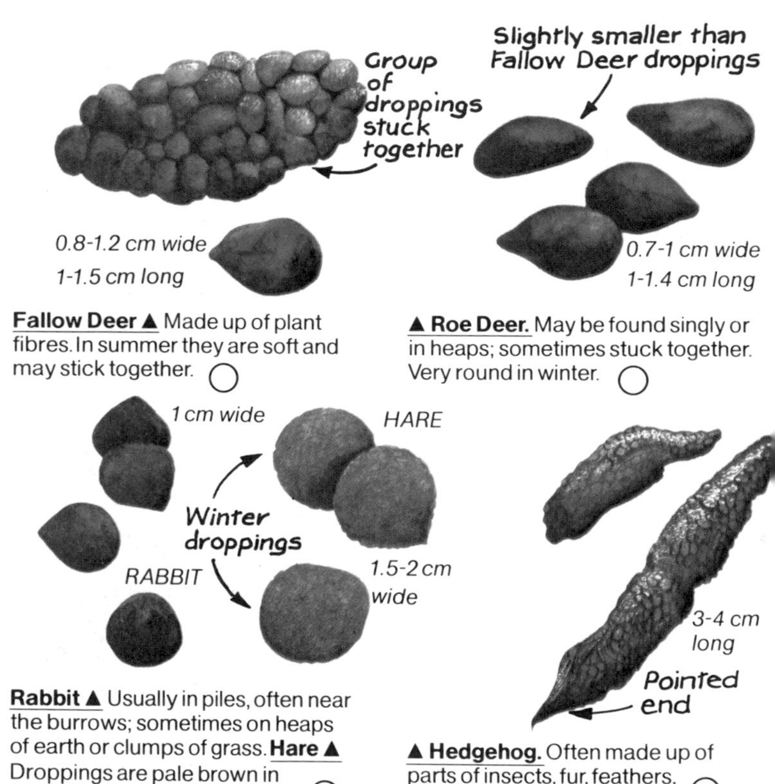

Fallow Deer ▲ Made up of plant fibres. In summer they are soft and may stick together. ◯

▲ Roe Deer. May be found singly or in heaps; sometimes stuck together. Very round in winter. ◯

Rabbit ▲ Usually in piles, often near the burrows; sometimes on heaps of earth or clumps of grass. **Hare ▲** Droppings are pale brown in winter, dark brown in summer. ◯

▲ Hedgehog. Often made up of parts of insects, fur, feathers, bones or remains of berries. ◯

Mammal droppings

Fox ► 7-10cm long. They may look like dog droppings but have a twisted point at one end. If they are grey they contain a lot of bone, but they are usually dark and may be made up of mice, birds, hard parts of insects, fruit and berries. They may be outside the den, or on clumps of grass or rocks. ○

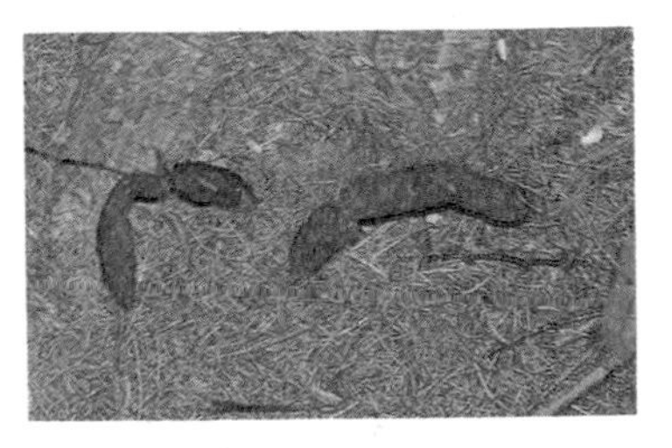

Badger droppings may be oval shaped or semi-liquid

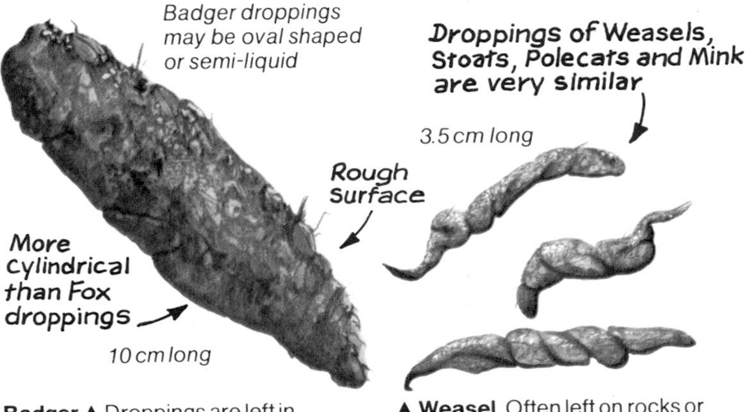

Badger ▲ Droppings are left in specially dug holes, about 10cm deep. They are not covered over. ○

▲ Weasel. Often left on rocks or clumps of grass. May contain fur, bones and feathers. ○

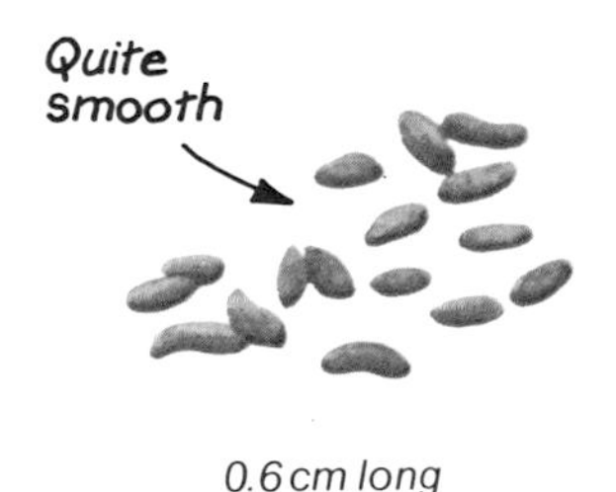

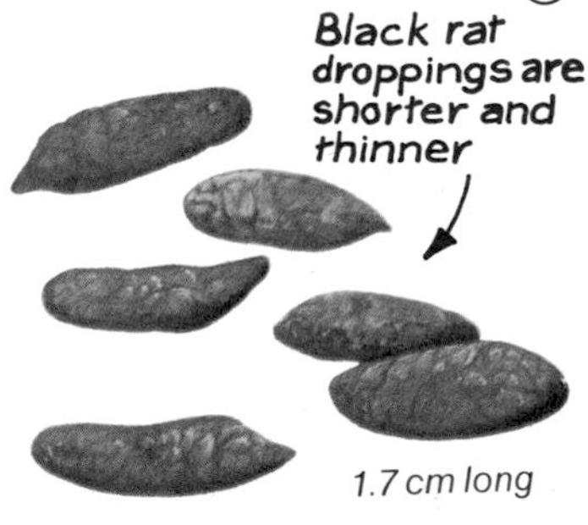

Field Vole ▲ Rather similar to mouse droppings. Greenish, or brown and made of plant remains. ○

▲ Brown Rat. Larger than Black Rat droppings. Left singly or in piles and made of plant remains. ○

Bird pellets and droppings

The food remains in the pellets you find may be different from the remains shown in the pellets on this page.

Pellets

A pellet is formed from the remains of food that the bird cannot digest. Instead of getting rid of it as a dropping, it coughs it up out of its beak. Pellets vary according to the size of the bird and the type of food it has been eating. Look for them at roosting, nesting or feeding places.

COMMON GULL

Very loose pellet; fish bones, plant remains

3.5–6 cm long

CROW

Grit, plant remains

3–4.5 cm long

▲Look for **gull pellets** in places where they may have been feeding. ◀ **Rook pellets** can be found under the nests of the rookery. ◀ **Crow pellets** are often found at their feeding places eg. fields.

ROOK

2–3 cm long

Grit, plant remains

SHORT-EARED OWL

4–9 cm long

Bird feathers and bones

4–7 cm long

LITTLE OWL

2.5 cm long

Insect remains bird feathers and bones

Owl pellets can be found ▶ under the owls' perching places. **Little Owls** often perch on posts and **Tawny Owls** in large trees in deciduous woods. **Barn Owl** pellets will be found under their nesting place.

BARN OWL

2–3 cm wide

4–6 cm long

Mammal fur and bones, feathers, bones of a small bird

TAWNY OWL

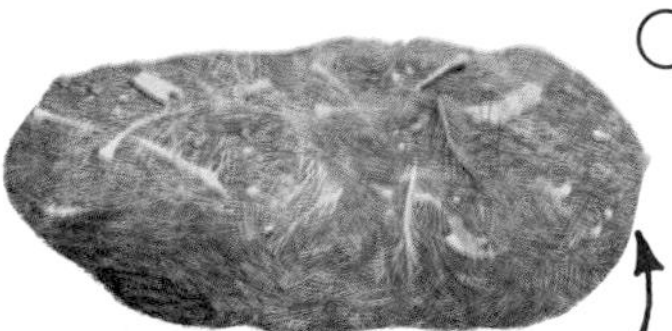

Feathers and bones of a bird

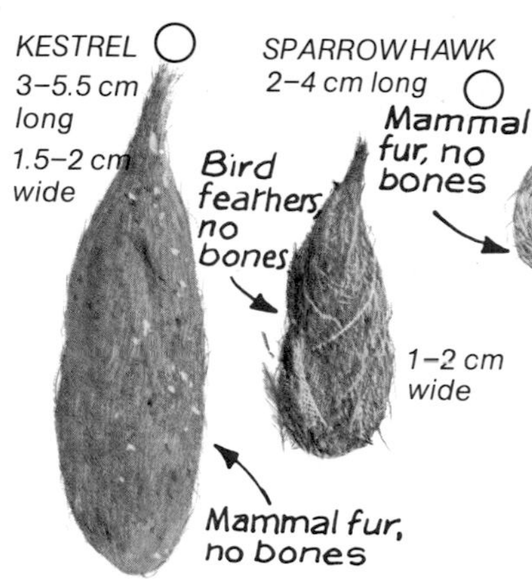

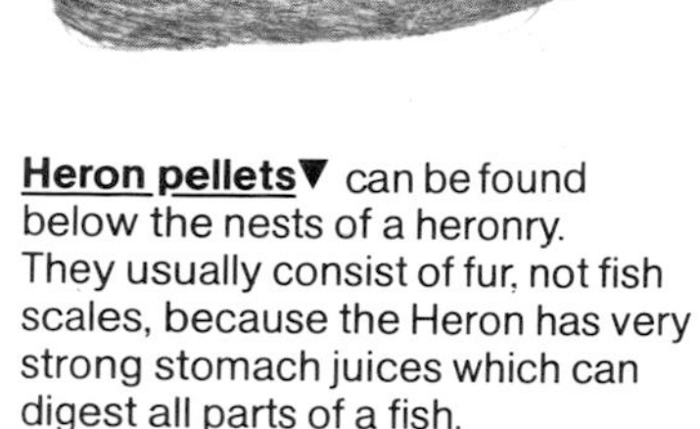

When feeding, **birds of prey** ▲ usually tear flesh and fur off the prey leaving any bones on the ground, therefore pellets do not often contain bones. Pellets can be found under fences, tree stumps or tall trees, where the birds may have been perching.

Heron pellets ▼ can be found below the nests of a heronry. They usually consist of fur, not fish scales, because the Heron has very strong stomach juices which can digest all parts of a fish.

Droppings

Bird urine (a whitish fluid) and faeces are usually mixed together as droppings. Birds which do not produce pellets get rid of any indigestible food, such as seeds of berries, in their droppings. There are three types of droppings, liquid ones, round, semi-firm ones, and long, firm ones.

▲ **Liquid Starling droppings.** Can be found at their feeding and roosting places and under nests.

Pheasant droppings ▲ The colour varies, but they usually have white urine at one end and are 2 cm long.

▲ **Goose droppings.** They are green, or grey-brown, 5-8 cm long and made of plant material.

Mammal homes above ground

Most hoofed animals do not have permanent homes. They sleep on the ground in sheltered places. The sleeping places of deer are called lairs; the vegetation here will be flattened and there may be droppings nearby. The Roe Deer scrapes away plants and twigs with its hooves before lying down. Other mammals, such as dormice, build nests in vegetation. The nests are well hidden and keep the animal warm and dry when it is sleeping. Different nests may be built in winter and summer; a nest which is used for breeding will be lined with soft material.

Old nests are easier to see in winter when the vegetation has died back. During breeding time, the activity of the parents popping in and out of the nest to feed young may lead you to the nest site. Do not remove any empty nests you find; they may be used. ○

Grey Squirrel's drey ▲ Made of twigs, lined with moss, grass, feathers and fur. Looks like a large, round bird's nest in the fork of a tree; a simple summer drey may be built on side branches. ○

▲ Harvest Mouse's summer nest Made of grass leaves woven around long grass or reed stems, high off the ground; sometimes in bushes. In winter, nests are in small tunnels, or under rocks or roots. ○

Dormouse's winter nest ▲ Made of plant material, mainly strips of bark. Found in thick undergrowth, often close to the ground, or in bushes especially hazel; sometimes in bird nesting boxes. ○

▲ Hare's form. A shallow hollow scraped away in earth, grass or snow, usually protected at the side by a clump of grass or a stone. The Hare sits with its hindquarters in the deepest part of the form. ○

Mammal homes below ground

Inside an underground burrow a mammal can keep warm and rear its young in safety. Signs outside the entrance, such as droppings or tracks, may tell you who lives inside; you should be able to guess the size of the owner from the size of the opening.

Each mammal has its own way of removing waste earth from the burrow. The Fox throws earth out of the entrance, leaving it in a fan-shaped pile; the Wood Mouse leaves a conical pile; the Mole pushes waste soil up onto the surface and the Water Vole presses it against the side of the burrow. ○

▲ **Molehills.** Made of waste earth from mole tunnels. The sleeping nest will be under the largest hill, called the fortress; this pile of earth may be over 30 cm high. The breeding nest will have no hill over it. ○

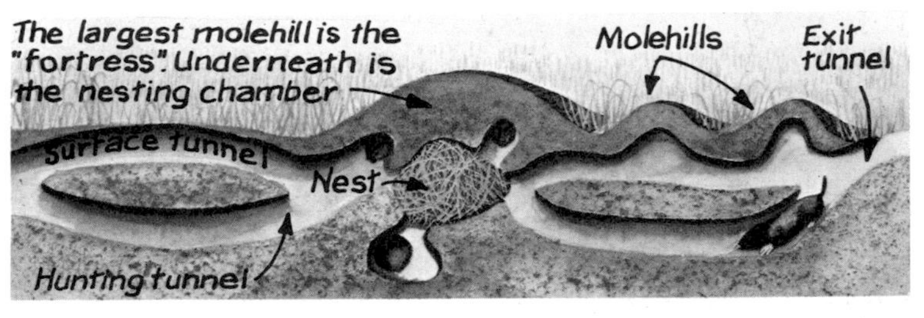

▲ **Fox's den.** Look for the heap of earth outside. There may be tracks or droppings on the earth and a strong smell inside the hole. Foxes often use badger sets or dig out old rabbit burrows. A single Fox, or a family of Foxes may live in each den. They may move dens. ○

Badger's set ▲ There may be remains of bedding outside the main entrance; other openings will be nearby. There is no smell inside the set and droppings are left in shallow holes outside. A group of Badgers will live in one set. ○

Mammal homes below ground

Rabbit burrows ▶ Rabbits usually live together in an underground warren which has many tunnels and lots of entrance holes. Holes that have been dug from the outside will have piles of earth outside them. There may be shallow scrapes (hollows) nearby and droppings near the holes. ○

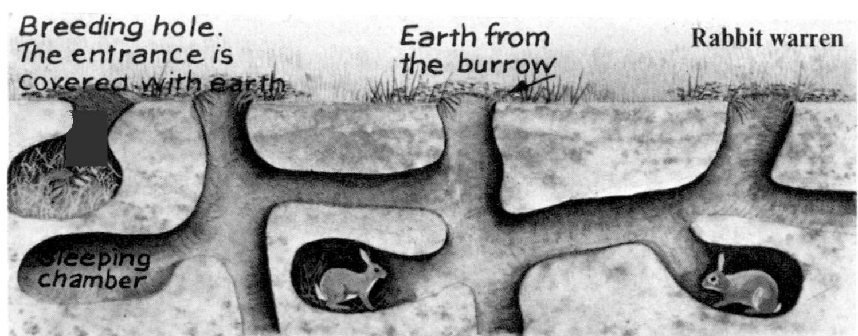

Water Vole's burrow ▼ ○

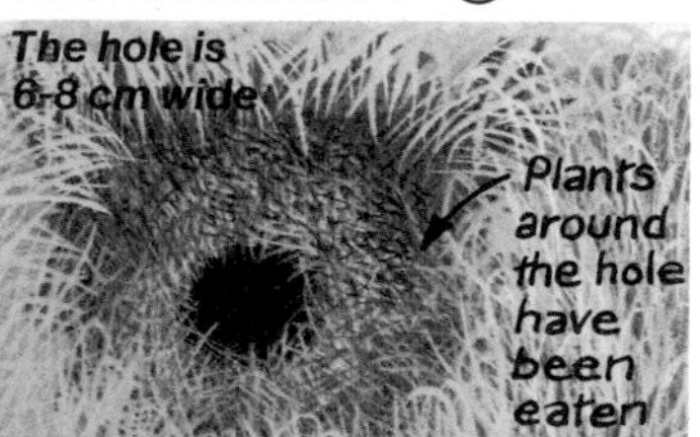

Wood Mouse's burrow ▼ ○

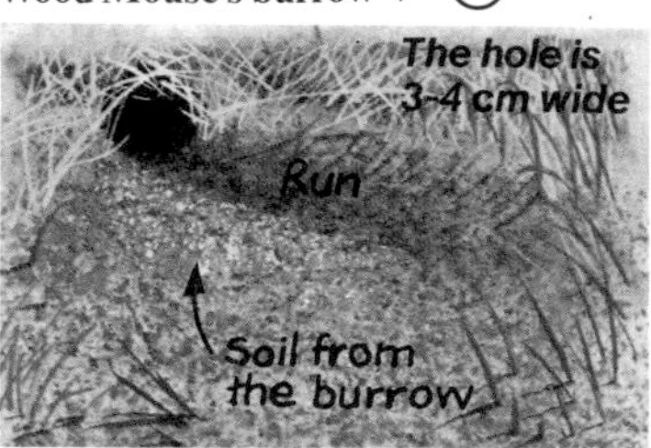

Rat's burrow ▼ ○

Measure any entrance holes you find and look for fresh tracks on the runs (paths). Holes made by Voles and mice are difficult to tell apart; also rat burrows on river banks are easily mistaken for Water Vole burrows; however, if the hole is just above the water, you can be sure it belongs to a Water Vole. Spider webs across a hole show that it is unused.

Bird nests

Nests are usually built in spring and summer. To protect the eggs against predators, the nest will be well hidden, or in a place which is difficult to reach (high in a tree, on water, or in a hole), or the eggs will be camouflaged. Some birds use the same nest each year, so only collect nests if you know they are old. Examine nests in autumn, when they will not contain young or eggs.

Lesser Black-backed Gull ▶ Ground nest with camouflaged eggs. Breeds May to June in colonies on cliffs, stony beaches or on moors. Nest is a shallow hollow lined with plant material.

◀ Green Woodpecker. Nest is hidden in a hole made by the bird, usually in a living tree. The hole is about 38cm deep and is from 1.5-15 metres up the tree. You may see wood chips underneath. The breeding season is from April to May. The hole may also be used for roosting.

Swallow ▶ Nest is high off the ground, stuck to a surface, usually on the wall under eaves of buildings or on rafters, sometimes under bridges. Nest is made of mud and bits of plants, lined with a few feathers. Breeding season is from May to June.

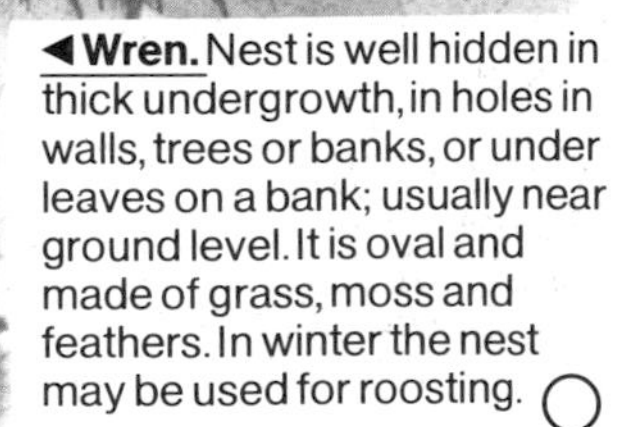

◀ Wren. Nest is well hidden in thick undergrowth, in holes in walls, trees or banks, or under leaves on a bank; usually near ground level. It is oval and made of grass, moss and feathers. In winter the nest may be used for roosting.

Bird nests

Long-tailed Tit ▶ Nest is well hidden in thick scrub, hedges, brambles, gorse, occasionally in trees. It is large, egg-shaped and made of moss woven with hairs and spiders' webs. It is lined with feathers and has lichen on the outside. Breeding season is March to April. ○

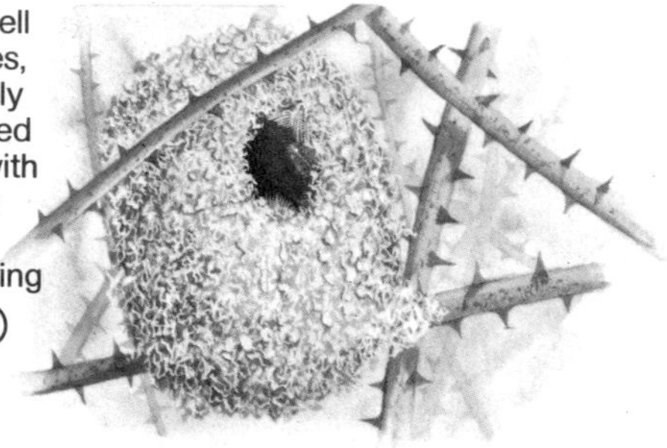

◀ **Song Thrush.** Nest is 1.5-3.5 metres off the ground, hidden in hedges, shrubs or trees, usually close to the trunk. Made of twigs, roots, grass, lichen, dead leaves and with a lining of mud. Breeding season is March to June. ○

Rook ▶ Nest is built in the top of a tree. Breeds in a colony called a rookery. Nest is made of sticks and earth, lined with plant material, wool and hair. The same nest may be used the following year; it may also be used for roosting. Breeding season is March to May. ○

◀ **Coot.** Nest is built among water plants in, or near water, on lakes, ponds and streams. It is made of stems of water plants and dead leaves. Breeding season is from March onwards. ○

Bats

All British and European bats feed on flying insects.

Pipistrelle Bat ▶

Rusty to dark brown back, yellow-brown belly. Common in open woods, town parks and squares, and villages. Rapid flight with jerky movements. Hibernates with others in hollow trees and buildings.
Wing span 20cm.
BL 5cm.

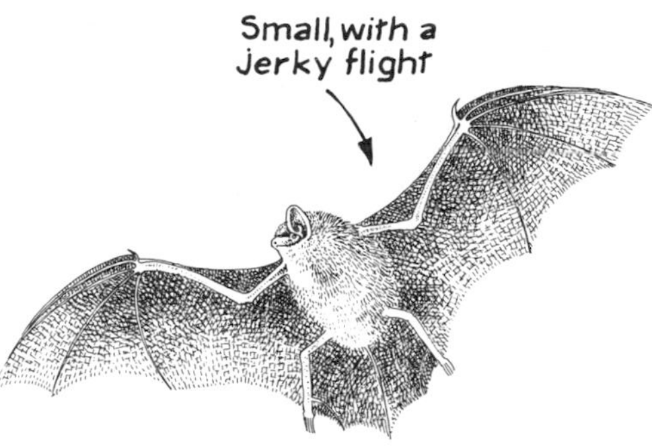

◀ Long-eared Bat

Yellow brown back, paler belly. Not very common. Seen in woodlands, orchards, often near buildings. Flies in the late evening. Hibernates in cellars, caves, mine-shafts. Ears fold up when it is at rest. Wing span 25cm.
BL 5cm.

Daubenton's/ Water Bat ▶

Reddish-brown back, dirty white belly. Common in some places, usually near water. Has a vibrating flight and may fly by day. Hibernates among rocks, cellars, roof-tops.
Wing span 24cm.
BL 4cm.

Bats

Noctule Bat ►

Reddish-brown back, paler belly. Seen in parks, woods and gardens; has a bold flight. Hibernates in trees and buildings.
Wing span 38cm.
BL 7cm.

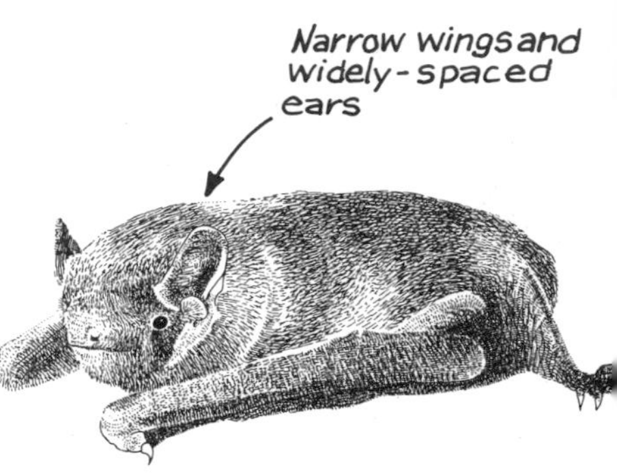

◄ Whiskered Bat

Fluttering flight and long body hair

Dark grey-brown back, greyish belly. Often seen flying low near water; has a fluttering flight. Hibernates in trees, caves, cellars. Males usually solitary.
Wing span 23cm.
BL 5cm.

Greater Horseshoe Bat ►

Grey-brown back, pale grey belly. Male is a reddish colour. More common in mountainous areas. Flies fairly low and may glide. Hibernates in rocks, caves, quarries, mine-shafts, hanging vertically from the roof. Protected by law in Britain.
Wing span 35cm.
BL 6cm.

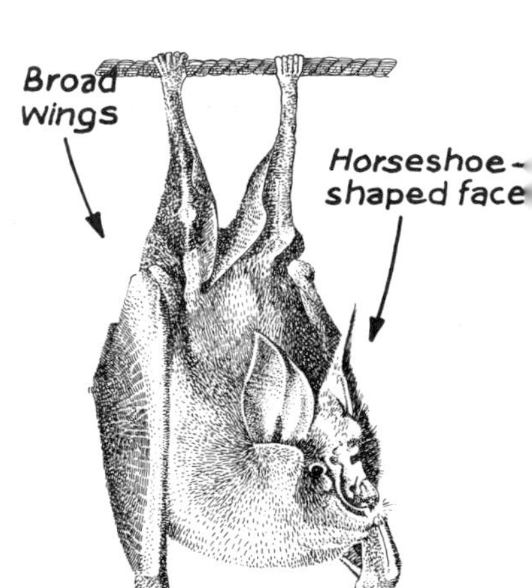

Studying owl pellets

Dissecting the pellet

First measure and weigh your pellet and write down the details. Now carefully break the pellet into two and place the pieces in the jug of water. Leave them for a couple of hours so the water has a chance to soak in, then gently shake the water. Remove any fur or feathers that float to the top and pour off the water. Add fresh water and repeat the process. Continue doing this until you are left with mostly bones. Pour off the water and empty the bones onto a kitchen towel on a saucer. Use the tweezers and needle to remove any bits that are still sticking to them. To clean the bones and make them white, leave them for a few minutes in hydrogen peroxide (you can get this from your chemist).

What you need ▲

Store the different types of bones in matchboxes. Write on a label where and when they were found and which pellet they came from.

Identifying the bones

You will be surprised at the number of bones you will find in just one pellet. They may come from several different animals, but you may be lucky and find enough bones to make up part of a skeleton. Identifying bones is difficult, but can be done if you have a good book. A special booklet is recommended in the book list on page 60.

Types of bones

Below you can see some of the common types of bones you will find. Most of them will be from shrews, mice and voles and small birds. You may also find some beetle wing-cases in the pellets.

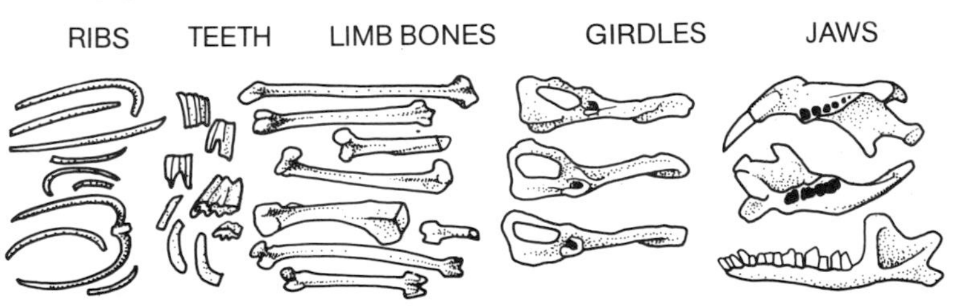

Making plaster casts of tracks

One of the best ways to make a record of tracks you have seen is to start a collection of casts of tracks. Casts give you an accurate record of the track and also look nice when they are painted and varnished.

Things you will need

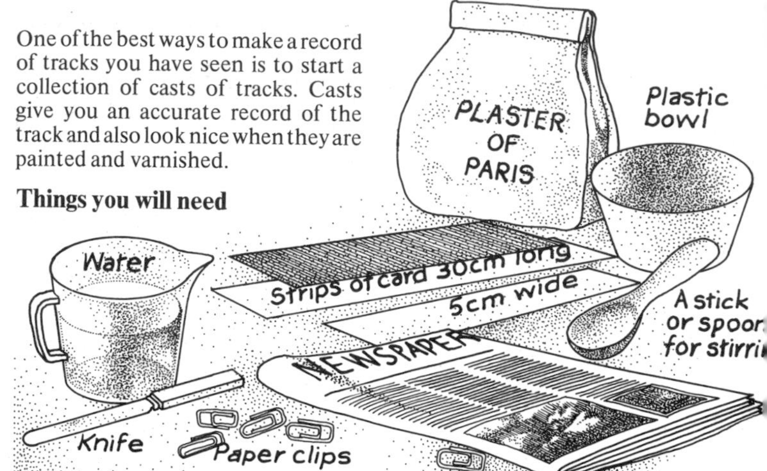

The picture above shows the equipment you will need. Buy the plaster of Paris from a chemist. When you go out, carry the powder and water in two screw-top jam jars with the lids tightly screwed on.

When you find a good track, take out one of the strips of card (they should be 30cm long and 5cm wide) and bend it round the track. Join the ends together with a paper clip. Push the card ring a little way into the ground.

Empty into the plastic bowl enough of the plaster of Paris powder to fill half the card ring, then carefully add water, a little at a time, stirring the mixture as you do this. Stop adding water when the mixture begins to feel like thin porridge.

Do not make the mixture too thick. Pour it into the card ring, being careful to pour it at the side of the track if the track is in dust.

Leave the cast to dry for at least 15 minutes, so it has time to set hard. You can leave it for longer if you want to make other casts nearby.

When the cast has set, use the knife to lift it up out of the ground. Brush off any mud on the cast and when you get home, carefully wash off the rest of the dirt using a soft toothbrush.

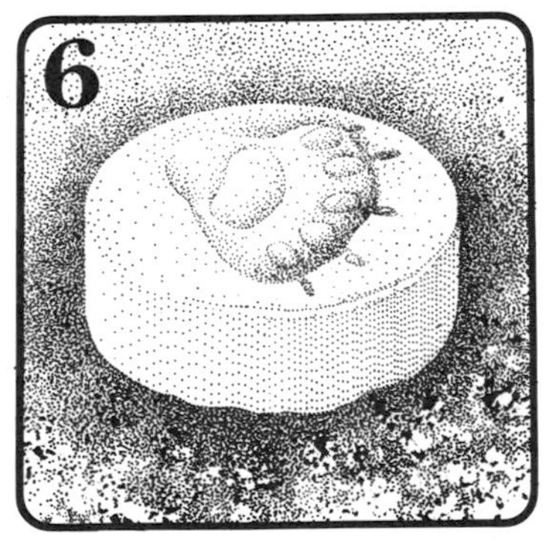

Wrap the cast in newspaper to carry it home. When it is clean you can paint the track to make it show up. Varnish the whole cast with clear varnish; this will protect it from scratches and dirt.

Displaying your collection

You can store your collection of finds in many different ways. Make sure your specimens (especially things like feet, skulls and pellets) are properly dried and clean or they will rot and have to be thrown away. Wrap fragile specimens in a little cotton wool and put them in small plastic bags tied with rubber bands.

Always label your finds clearly. A collection without labels means very little, but with labels it is of real scientific interest. You can use name tags or sticky labels. If you find a chewed cone, or a nibbled nut and you cannot identify the animal that has handled it, label it with the date and place where you found it. Look it up in one of the books listed on page 60, or take it to your local museum to be identified.

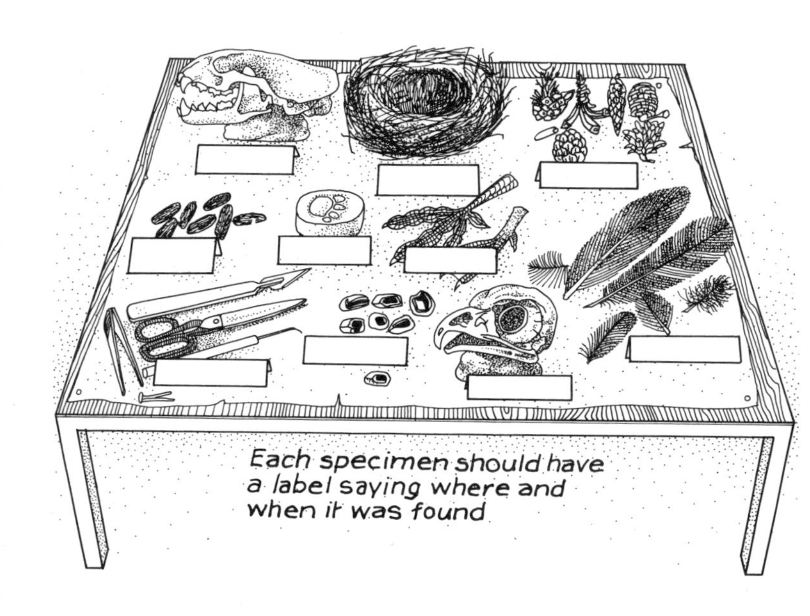

Nature Table

You can make your own nature table at home. If there is no spare table use shelves, or make shelves out of orange boxes nailed together. Make the display as attractive as possible. Use coloured labels or make stands for each exhibit out of coloured plasticine. Stick small things such as snail shells onto card so they do not get knocked off the table and broken.

Once you start building up a big collection you will not have room to display everything on one table. Below are some ideas for storing smaller objects.

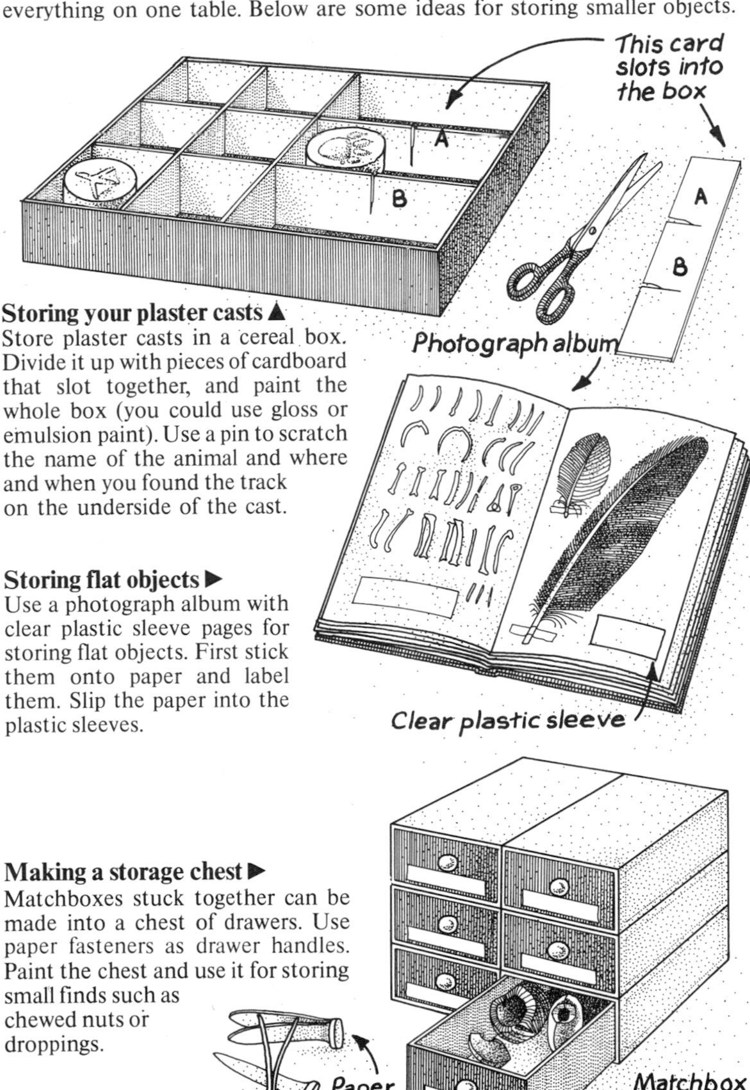

Storing your plaster casts ▲

Store plaster casts in a cereal box. Divide it up with pieces of cardboard that slot together, and paint the whole box (you could use gloss or emulsion paint). Use a pin to scratch the name of the animal and where and when you found the track on the underside of the cast.

Storing flat objects ►

Use a photograph album with clear plastic sleeve pages for storing flat objects. First stick them onto paper and label them. Slip the paper into the plastic sleeves.

Making a storage chest ►

Matchboxes stuck together can be made into a chest of drawers. Use paper fasteners as drawer handles. Paint the chest and use it for storing small finds such as chewed nuts or droppings.

Watching mammals

What to take

Wear dull coloured clothes and a hat to cover your forehead. Take a notebook and pencil, waterproofs, something waterproof to sit on and if possible, a pair of binoculars.

Where to go

The best times to go out are in the early morning and evening when the animals are active. Choose a quiet spot. Woods are good places for larger mammals; you can also see or hear small mammals like voles and shrews in banks and hedges. Look for burrows and holes. The best time to watch burrows is in the early evening when most animals come out to feed. If you live in a town, your local park may have deer, hedgehogs, or squirrels which you could study.

Stalking animals

Test which way the wind is blowing and walk into the wind so that the animals do not catch your scent. Keep to trees and bushes and move quietly and slowly. Never make sudden movements. Do not walk along a ridge, because the animals will see your outline against the sky.

Making a hide

If you know where an animal lives and want to watch it unseen, build a hide. It should blend in with the surroundings, be large enough for you to sit in and have a small slit in the front which you can see through. Make a wigwam frame of sticks tied together at the top with string. Cover it with dull coloured material and try to camouflage it with leaves and branches. Leave some material loose at the back for the entrance. Build it the day before you want to use it so that the animal can get used to the new smell.

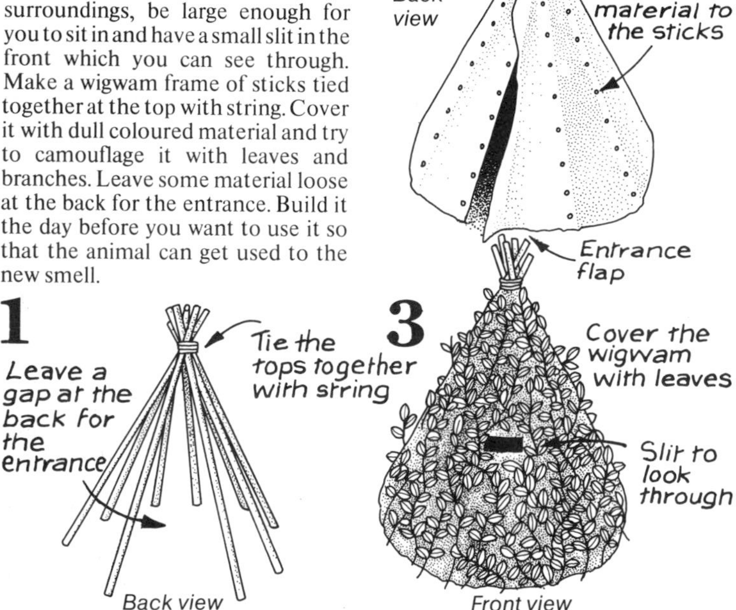

Tips on photography

Taking photos of animals is not easy, so do not be disappointed if your first pictures are bad. The more you practise, the better you will become; you will learn from making mistakes.

The camera

Professional nature photographers use special cameras with telescopic attachments (telephoto lenses) for taking pictures of animals in the distance, and magnifying attachments (close-up lenses) for taking pictures of very small objects. However, this kind of equipment is expensive and you can take reasonable pictures with a little instamatic camera which is simple to use and can be fitted with a flash cube.

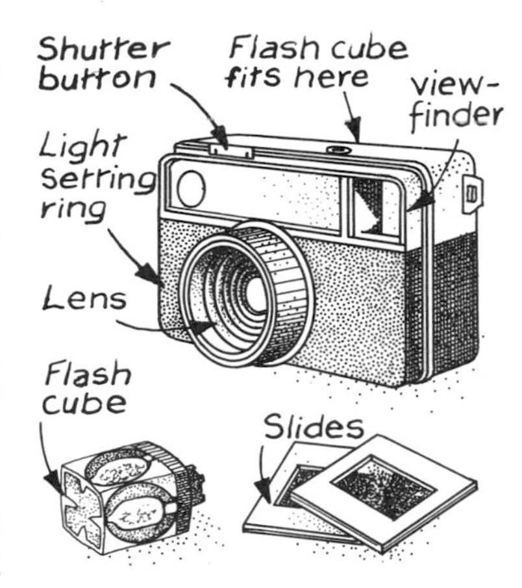

The film

Black and white film is fine for taking photos of tracks, but you really need colour for animal photos. Buy colour slide film rather than colour print film as it is cheaper to develop. Take several photos of each subject in case the first one does not work.

Mistakes you may make ▼

The animal was too far away

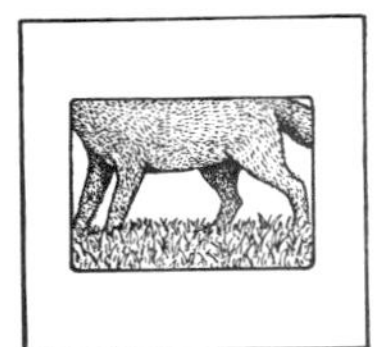

You did not look through the viewfinder properly

The animal moved

What have you got in the picture?

Unless you are very lucky, most animals you see will be at a distance. Check through the viewfinder before taking the photo that the animal is not just a dot in the picture. If it is fairly close, check that it is in the centre of the picture and that you have not cut off its head or tail.

Movement

If you shake when taking the photo, jolt the camera, or if the animal moves, the picture will come out blurred. Remember that when you are taking photos there is more chance of the animal seeing you when you move to bring the camera up to your eye.

Light

Your camera will have a light setting ring which can be adjusted for sunny days, cloudy days, or rainy, dark days. Check to see if the ring is in the right position before taking a photo. If you are somewhere dark, like a wood, turn the ring to the rainy position. If the wood is very dark, or it is evening time, use a flash cube. They are quite cheap to buy and fit onto the camera.

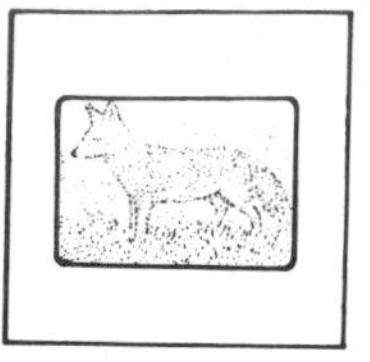

Your setting dial was in the wrong position. The photo is over-exposed

It was too dark when you took the photograph

Making notes

After you have taken the photo, note down its number, what the subject was, how far away it was, the light conditions and the light setting you used. If you take a bad photo, your notes may give you an idea about what went wrong. When the photos are developed, mark on them the date and subject.

Noise

If you want to study the animal for a time, remember that the shutter of the camera will make a clicking noise when you take the photo and may scare the animal away. A flash will also frighten the animal.

Photographing tracks and signs

Try to take photos of tracks in early evening when the sun is at an angle; this will throw a shadow onto the outline of the track and make it more visible. Take any flash pictures at a slight angle, instead of directly above the track, so that the rim of the track nearest to you will be in shadow.

Always put something next to the track or sign to show the scale of the object. Use a coin if you have not got a ruler with you. If you are taking a photo of something on the ground, remember to move away any plants that may be hiding it.

With an instamatic camera you cannot take a photo any less than one metre from the subject. If you want to take pictures of small things like nuts, you will need a more expensive camera.

Put something next to the track or sign to show the scale

Glossary

Camouflage - colouring pattern making an animal or object difficult to see.
Canine teeth - long and pointed, usually one on each side of the upper and lower jaws.
Carnivore - meat eater. Also the name of a large group of animals which includes bears, dogs, cats, weasels and their relatives. Most are meat eaters, but some, eg. bears, also eat plant material.
Cleaves - the two parts of a deer's hoof.
Colony - a group of animals living together.
Conifer wood - made up of conifer trees which usually have narrow, needle-like, or scaly leaves and produce fruit enclosed in cones.
Copse - small wood, usually with lots of undergrowth.
Deciduous wood - made up of trees which drop their leaves in autumn.
Decomposition - when substances rot and are broken down into simpler substances.
Den - home of a fox.
Dew claw - inner claw and toe, usually higher up the foot than other toes and reduced in size.
Domestic animals - animals kept by man.
Estuary - mouth of a large river. Fresh water is mixed with sea water and at low tide large areas of mud are exposed.
Ewe - female sheep.
Game Birds - ground-living birds, hunted by man eg. Pheasant.
Girdles - shoulder or hip bones.
Hibernation - when animals sleep through the cold winter period. Their temperature falls and they do not eat.
Hind - female Red Deer.
Incisor teeth - flat, long, sharp teeth at the front of the mouth.
Insectivores - a group of animals which eat insects.
Kernel - the soft part of the seed inside a nut.
Lagomorphs - hares and rabbits.
Larva - the form which some animals take before they become adult, eg. the caterpillar form of a butterfly.
Lichen - small, dry-looking plants, rather like mosses.
Migration - movement of animals to another area, usually far away.
Molar teeth - back teeth, used for crushing food; they usually have flat, ridged surfaces.
Nocturnal - active mostly at night.
Omnivore - eats anything.
Perching place - where a bird sits to feed or rest.
Predator - an animal which kills and eats other animals.
Preening - when a bird cleans and oils its feathers.
Rodents - a group of animals with long teeth for gnawing, eg. mice.
Roosting place - perching place where a bird sleeps.
Rut - mating period of deer and other hoofed animals.
Set - home of a badger.
Solitary - living alone.
Stag - male deer.
Territory - some animals defend part of the area in which they live; this is their territory.
Tundra - cold, treeless area in the Arctic.
Ungulate - hoofed animal.
Vegetarian - plant eating animal.
Waterfowl - birds which spend a lot of time on water, eg. ducks.

Books to read

The Nature Trail Book of Wild Animals. R. Harthill (Usborne Publishing). This book describes how mammals live.
A Field Guide to the Mammals of Britain and Europe. F. H. Van Den Brink (Collins). Detailed descriptions and good illustrations; has photos of skulls.
Mammals of Britain; Their Tracks, Trails and Signs. M. J. Lawrence and R. W. Brown (Blandford). Has detailed descriptions of all the mammals and shows their tracks. Worth buying.
Animal Tracks and Signs. P. Bang and P. Dahlstrom (Collins). The best book for animal signs with lots of photographs. Worth buying.
Finding and identifying mammals in Britain. G. B. Corbet (British Museum - Natural History). Small, useful guide with notes about skulls and teeth. Cheap.
A Field Guide to the Birds of Britain and Europe. R. T. Peterson, G. Mountford and P. A. D. Hollom (Collins). Good field guide.
David Stephen's Guide to Watching Wildlife. (Collins). Many interesting tips. Cheap.
Illustrated Teach Yourself Watching Wildlife. R. Philps (Hodder & Stoughton). Useful, easy to read and cheap.
Foxes. A. Bartram (Priory Press). This is one of the Young Naturalist series of books which includes other titles such as *Squirrels* and *Bats.* You should be able to borrow all these books from your library.
The identification of remains in owl pellets. D. W. Yalden (The Mammal Society). Very useful.
First Guide to Cameras and Photographs. P. Hawksby (Usborne Publishing). Useful little guide for beginners.

Clubs to join

The Council for Environmental Conservation (address: Zoological Gardens, Regent's Park, London NW1 4RY) will supply the addresses of your local **Natural History Societies.** (Send a stamped, addressed envelope for a free list.) Many of these have specialist sections and almost all have field meetings. **The Royal Society for Nature Conservation** (address: 22, The Green, Nettleham, Lincoln LN2 2NR) will give you the address of your **County Naturalist Trust,** which may have a junior branch. Many of the Trusts have meetings, lectures, and opportunities for work on reserves.

The British Naturalists' Association will have a branch in your area and has a quarterly magazine with a special section for junior members. For details, write to Mrs Y. Griffiths, 23 Oak Hill Close, Woodford Green, Essex IG8 9PH.

If you are interested in local field work and in making surveys of the mammals in your area, join the **Mammal Society.** Write to Ms Lenton (address: 5 Stephens Court, Bath, Avon) for information about youth membership. Visit your local museum which will have a section on mammals.

Scorecard

The animals in this scorecard are arranged in alphabetical order. When you see an animal or a track made by the animal, fill in the date next to its name. The scores for animal signs, such as droppings and nests, are arranged alphabetically in their own section at the end of the scorecard. You can add up your score after a day out spotting.

	Score	Date seen		Score	Date seen
Badger	15		Deer, Sika	15	
Bat, Daubenton's	15		Dog, Domestic	5	
Bat, Greater Horseshoe	20		Dormouse, Common	20	
Bat, Long-eared	15		Dormouse, Edible	20	
Bat, Noctule	10		Dormouse, Garden	25	
Bat, Pipistrelle	10		Duck, Mallard	5	
Bat, Whiskered	15		Elk	25	
Bear, Brown	25		Fox, Arctic	25	
Beaver	25		Fox, Red	10	
Boar, Wild	25		Goat, Domestic	10	
Cat, Domestic	5		Goose, Greylag	15	
Cat, Wild	20		Grebe, Great Crested	20	
Chamois	25		Gull, Herring	5	
Coot	5		Hamster, European	25	
Cormorant	10		Hare, Blue	15	
Cow, Domestic	5		Hare, Brown	5	
Coypu	20		Hedgehog	10	
Curlew	15		Heron, Grey	15	
Deer, Fallow	10		Ibex	25	
Deer, Red	15		Lemming, Norway	25	
Deer, Roe	15		Lynx	25	

	Score	Date seen
Marmot, Alpine	25	
Marten, Beech	25	
Marten, Pine	20	
Mink	15	
Mole	10	
Moorhen	5	
Mouflon	25	
Mouse, Harvest	20	
Mouse, House	5	
Mouse, Wood	10	
Mouse, Yellow-necked Field	15	
Muntjac	20	
Muskrat	25	
Otter	20	
Pheasant	10	
Pig, Domestic	5	
Polecat	20	
Pony, Exmoor	10	
Rabbit	5	
Rat, Common	5	

	Score	Date seen
Rat, Ship	25	
Reindeer	15	
Rook	5	
Seal, Common	10	
Seal, Grey	15	
Sheep, Domestic	5	
Shrew, Common	10	
Shrew, Pygmy	15	
Shrew, Water	15	
Shrew, White-toothed	25	
Sparrow, House	5	
Squirrel, Grey	5	
Squirrel, Red	15	
Stoat	15	
Vole, Bank	10	
Vole, Field	5	
Vole, Water	15	
Weasel	15	
Wolf	25	

Scorecard

Animal signs

	Score	Date seen		Score	Date seen
Bird beaks	20		Mammal homes above ground	20	
Bird droppings	5		Mammal homes below ground	10	
Bird nests	10		Mammal skulls	20	
Bird pellets	20		Meal remains of meat eaters	25	
Droppings	10		Meal remains of plant eaters	15	
Fir cones eaten by animals	15		Nuts eaten by animals	15	
Fur and feathers	5				

Index

If an animal's name is in **bold type**, it shows that there is a picture of the animal and its track in the main section of the book; if the name appears in ordinary type, the animal is not illustrated, but some of its signs and tracks are.